Look at America

BY THE EDITORS OF LOOK

Look at America

THE COUNTRY YOU KNOW—AND DON'T KNOW

HOUGHTON MIFFLIN COMPANY · BOSTON

The Riverside Press

a LOOK PICTURE BOOK

HOUGHTON MIFFLIN COMPANY, BOSTON, MASS. THE RIVERSIDE PRESS

Contents

Introduction

ENERGY. THAT IS AMERICA in a word. Observers sensed this from the beginning. "An immense vitality animates this growing state," wrote Baron de Neuville to a friend in Europe in 1807. "One feels, on taking a near view of America, as if something unknown were stirring in the future . . . as if a fresh breeze had passed over the world. . . . It seems, sometimes, as if America had surprised the secret and forestalled the hour."

That was nearly a century and a half ago, when it took days to travel from, say, Boston to New York; when movement from one part of the country to another was slow and hazardous. Yet De Neuville's remarks are appropriate today, when any part of the country can be reached by airplane in a few hours. Today a web of steel and concrete obliterates distance, facilitating the exchange of goods and persons between regions. Raw materials go a thousand miles by rail and water to the factory, come back another thousand as finished products. More rapidly still, radio and telephones reach into the remotest hamlet. Differences of climate and background begin to lose significance. Despite the country's size, the life of the whole nation is as closely integrated today as was the life of a single state in the eighteenth century.

The drive needed to achieve this integration was manifest in the men and women who settled America. It required determination and audacity to leave the comparative security of Europe and make a living on the shores of New England and Virginia. It took initiative and self-reliance to push the frontier to the west, north and south, to thrust long ribbons across the plains, over mountains and through deserts, to reach the Pacific coast, to feed settlers in increasing numbers till the tide flooded and rolled back to fill the intervening sections where it was thought no man could live. It required fervor and imagination to seek different ways of finding God, here imposing the rigid patterns of Puritanism; there reacting violently in dramatic counter-currents; elsewhere revealing a tolerance generally unfamiliar in Europe.

Enterprise and temerity were needed to uncover and exploit the resources of the land — the plains that nourished great herds, the prairies that made possible huge farms, the seemingly limitless forests, the coal, the iron ore, the copper, the oil. Imagination and resourcefulness

7

were needed for inventions to make possible the development of industries, to make America the nation where the machine age finds its fullest expression. Faith and enthusiasm were needed to work out a concept of democracy in which every man should have the opportunity to better himself.

Such extremes of effort and initiative affected the temperament of Americans. Many derive satisfaction from going somewhere in a hurry, without inquiring too closely what they will do when they get there; from intensifying their efforts without asking whether those efforts are really worth while. Our contemporary civilization, it has been claimed, has "made the world safe for stupidity." Certainly many of us have been fascinated by flagpole sitters, marathon dancers, goldfish swallowers and soap-bubble blowers. We devote a considerable part of our energy to absorbing comics and "soap operas." There is also a hectic side to our animation which occasionally breaks out in a ferment of violence and gangsterism. There are the shattered nerves which send increasing numbers of Americans into sanitariums. The soberer citizens, meanwhile, crowd into cities, there spend a lifetime in order to possess ever bigger and handsomer appurtenances. Household gadgets are streamlined; a new, shiny car is more important than a place to live.

Yet, having achieved the conquest and development of a continent, America today holds world leadership in its grasp. And, as if for the first time, the nation gropes toward the spiritual, seeking a way of life it can pass on to others.

The early Americans came from western Europe, and our civilization is patterned on that of western Europe — of Britain, if you will. But what a difference! The western European was the leader of the world for centuries and has imposed his pattern well-nigh universally. However, he became the product of an ancient, exhausted, fatigued and cynical civilization. If the first settlers in America thought of the country as a larger, more spacious and perhaps superior Europe, they did not reckon with the land itself. Gradually, relentlessly, a primitive, elemental country set its mark on them. They lost the stigma of age and acquired the fire of youth. They even lost some of the virtues of age and acquired some of the faults of youth. Out of the western European, transplanted to a new world, a new man was forged: the American.

Take such a relatively uncomplicated factor as climate. In America "the somer is hot as is Spaine; the winter colde as in France or England," wrote Captain John Smith, adding, "Here the proverbe is true that no extreame long continueth." In England there is a range of from eleven to twenty degrees between mean temperatures of the coldest and hottest months of the year. In Minneapolis, the normal average for January is 13 degrees, for July, 72 degrees. Western Europe is characterized as a rule by soft skies and gradual changes, but it is commonplace for Americans suddenly to find themselves "wearing the wrong clothes." Buffeted by alternate waves of scorching heat and biting cold, driving wind and sopping rain, flared at by lightning and growled at by thunderstorms, the inhabitants of this continent are lucky if they do not at some time meet a blizzard, an earthquake, a tornado or a tidal wave. The swift variability and invigorating briskness of the climate are reflected in the American temperament.

As between Europe and America, the meaning of the word "frontier" itself is illuminating. To the citizen of the Old World it calls up striped sentry boxes, soldiers, police, immi-

8

Grand Canyon, Arizona

gration and customs inspectors who might speak another language. It reminds him that, across the barrier, lie the cities and towns of another country. To the American, the frontier has meant the edge of his own civilization, with beyond it the wilderness, the unknown — pregnant with possibilities, full of opportunity.

One of the greatest contrasts between the U. S. and countries in western Europe is in size. If a family living in Woonsocket, Rhode Island, decided to visit the West Coast, the trip might well take three weeks of driving forty hours a week at an average of thirty miles an hour. In their wanderings they would pass forests of factory chimneys, trim rows of commuters' houses, cities packed with office buildings scraping the clouds, cities with dignified government buildings in the classic style. They would see fertile valleys, placid rivers, stretches of deep woods, productive prairies, arid plains, rolling hills, mountains with peaks mantled in snow, shining lakes, waterfalls like bridal veils, bone-dry deserts, inland seas big enough to hide the navies of the world and, finally, a sunlit ocean whose farther edge touches the coast of Cathay.

Chances are they would see hundreds of types of human beings — a corporation lawyer on his way to a directors' meeting, a Kentucky mountaineer tipping his chair back against the wall, his rifle on his knees. They would see farmers, miners, lumberjacks, truck-gardeners, fishermen, cowboys; men with red skins, men with black skins; men in fedoras, Panamas, derbies, Stetsons, sombreros and feather bonnets.

Yet all the time the family from Woonsocket would be in the same country, subject to the same laws and regulations, among people who speak the same language and who in the main fit into the same cultural pattern.

But if, say, a retired bullfighter living outside of Cadiz, Spain, decided to visit Russia and he and his family traveled at about the same speed for about the same length of time as the American family, the Spaniards might get well beyond Leningrad and even end up at Archangel or Murmansk, on the extreme northern edge of eastern Europe. In the course of their travels they might pass through ten different countries most of which have different laws and different police systems; with inhabitants speaking different tongues and having widely different temperaments. Until they crossed the boundary separating western Europe from Russia, it is unlikely that they would traverse any really extensive stretches of forest or prairie on the North American scale.

But size alone does not account for the greatness of the United States, which is smaller than Canada or Brazil and less than half the size of Russia. In addition to a national domain of vast extent, there must be a wealth of natural resources. Nor is this enough. The resources must be exploited. Products must be marketed. This necessitates a flourishing industrial set-up; a large population living on a scale that permits the people to consume products of farm and factory; a stable government capable of guiding the national economy. Even before Europe was ravaged by a second World War, only Russia could compete with the United States in these respects, and Russia is less integrated, less evolved industrially and politically.

Symbols of pre-eminence are everywhere at hand to help the traveler understand America. Consider, for example, the significance of the skyscrapers of New York in typifying the bigness, the ascendancy of America. One might well ask why America produced a city whose buildings

10

are so tall and so many that its sky line is one of the wonders of the world. The answer is that the economic power of the United States was concentrated to such an extent on the surface of Manhattan Island that land values became exorbitant. The only direction buildings could take in expanding was a vertical one.

This humming hive, this busy city-state, with news agencies, radio networks and the entire entertainment industry (with the exception of the movies) centralized in its towers, with also a major part of the nation's publishing, artistic and educational endeavors, is a focal point for ideas.

But New York is more. In its roadstead merchant ships from all over the world ride at anchor; sleek liners are warped to its piers. It is one of the great harbors of the world, symbol of the fact that the broad Atlantic is an avenue of exchange and trade between the Old World and the New.

If New York is the focal point for the ideas and commerce of the nation, Washington is the focal point for its policies as well as its rumors. Colonnaded monuments and dignified Greek buildings lining the stately avenues laid out by Major L'Enfant may remind the more thoughtful sightseer that the United States has a form of government which, with all its imperfections, has perhaps been better able than any other to stimulate, guide, control and above all integrate the economy of a powerful nation.

Beyond the cities there are solid examples of factors that have made America great. The prosperous farms of the Pennsylvania Dutch, with their big barns and well-kept fields, suggest that in the Keystone State lies some of the richest farm land in the world. In the mountains of West Virginia, the seams that ring the slopes, the ribbons of steel tracks point up the fact that the United States mines over two fifths of the world's coal and possesses half the world's coal reserves. The chant of the tobacco auctioneer at Lexington in Kentucky suggests that the U. S. produces roughly a third of the world's tobacco. Fields bordering a drive leading to some porticoed mansion reminiscent of the Old South symbolize the fact that half the cotton in the world is grown between the Ohio River and the Gulf of Mexico.

Long stretches of deep woods on the slopes of the Appalachians are part of the country's great timber resources. There are forests again in the Ozarks, in the peninsulas abutting on the Great Lakes, in the great stands of spruce and fir in Oregon and Washington and in the vaulted corridors of California's redwoods and sequoias.

Giant dams harness great rivers and produce power for significant experiments in public control of utilities. The United States possesses an estimated sixty-three million kilowatts of feasible hydroelectric power, in comparison to its present annual production of 11 million kilowatts, already far higher per capita than that of any other nation. At present it generates a third of the world's electric power.

As one speeds down a concrete highway through the heart of the Kansas prairie, with the speedometer pointing steadily at fifty-five, a lesson can be read in the sea of grain that reaches unbroken to the horizon. One sees why large-scale farming is practicable in America, why the U. S. leads the world in the production of farm machinery, why the Midwest is a granary surpassing the Ukraine in productivity. The fertile and varied soils of the United States

12

yield half the world's corn crop and roughly a quarter of all the world's cereals.

Oil wells, so common in Oklahoma that they crowd into the cities, recall that the United States and its possessions produce nearly two thirds of the world's supply.

The great iron mines of northern Michigan and Minnesota are reminders that more than a quarter of the known iron ore of the world is to be found within the continental limits of the United States, which mines and consumes roughly a third of the world's output. Heavily laden ore boats creeping along the shores of the Great Lakes and smoking chimneys of blast furnaces in the Central Northeast and Midwest testify that the United States produces at least a third of the world's pig iron and more than half its steel. The manufacture of automobiles, trucks and buses is the nation's biggest industry; Americans make more than three fifths of the world's motor vehicles.

Automobiles require highways, and it is not surprising to find that the United States has a third of all highway mileage. It also has more than a third of the world's railroad tracks, carrying more than a third of the world's freight tonnage. Three quarters of all mail is handled by the United States Post Office. A fifth of all telegraph messages go over the nation's wires. It has nearly three fifths of the world's telephone instruments and the same proportion of the world's telephone lines.

Indeed, its transportation and communication facilities make the U. S., despite its size, one of the most closely knit nations in the world. The rising flow of traffic of all kinds ignores the boundaries of states. Fat hogs from Iowa travel hundreds of miles by rail to packing plants of Kansas City or Chicago and emerge again as the contents of cans or barrels, to be loaded in other freight cars and rolled other hundreds of miles to jobbing centers, thence to shelves of a corner grocery in some small town. Every month thousands of freight cars shift the cereals and livestock and wool of the Midwestern prairies and upland ranges, the lumber of the Pacific Northwest. Vessels on the Great Lakes distribute their heavy cargoes of raw materials; from factories everywhere come finished products for the consumer. Freighters with cotton and rice ply the coastal routes. Increasingly, perishable commodities are rushed by air from one end of the continent to the other. The ups and downs of the California fruit pickers, the salmon canners of the Northwest, the miners of West Virginia, lumberjacks of the north woods and mill hands of the industrial South have their repercussions throughout the country. Interdependence spells integration. Americans have no difficulty in thinking of themselves as one nation.

Taken symbolically, almost everything the traveler sees can in some way be related to one or more of the factors establishing America's pre-eminence: the pioneer spirit of enterprise; the vast extent of the national domain; a geographical orientation favoring interchange with Europe; a varied, propitious climate; fertility of soil; staggering richness in major raw materials; the tools of production; the means of distribution; a great progressive population of diverse backgrounds and capabilities; widespread educational facilities; a stable, relatively efficient democratic government; an accumulation of capital. Another factor comes to mind: the ramparts of the Atlantic and Pacific oceans. Americans have an advantage over Europeans in that they have not been engaged in the fearsome task of destroying one another at frequent intervals.

14

Monument Valley, Utah

To look at America is not necessarily to understand it. Geography alone—the lay of the land—tells only part of the story. It is not enough to be aware of the fact that the United States is a broad, more or less rectangular band of territory three million square miles in extent, sweeping across the entire continent of North America, occupying, north and south, twenty-five degrees of latitude at the most favorable distance from the equator, with broad oceans to the east and west, an arm of the ocean to the south; with a chain of five huge northern lakes linked to the eastern ocean by a waterway and to the southern gulf by a great river bisecting the continent. It is still not enough to know that the nation is traversed by great mountain ranges in the East and West, between which lies a broad, gently rising plain a thousand miles wide and a thousand miles deep.

Perhaps a better way to understand America is to think of it as a group of regions. "If I had to sum up my impressions," declared Sir William Beveridge, English political leader best known to Americans as the sponsor of the Beveridge Plan, "I should think in terms of drama; I should choose a parody from Pirandello: 'Six Americas in search of a faith.' " Given our preoccupation with the material aspects of life, it is not necessarily certain that the nation's great regions are consciously seeking a philosophy, nor that we need to find one to achieve unity. But it is certain that geography has divided the country up into great regions which have divergent ways of living and thinking, different racial origins and background, different pasts and different economic interests.

Sociologists and geographers agree that the number of regions into which the country seems naturally to divide are six or seven:

The Central Northeast includes the greatest metropolis, New York, which may become the capital of the world. It contains Washington, the seat of the national government. It contains Philadelphia, city of tolerance, of William Penn and Benjamin Franklin. It contains Pittsburgh, which epitomizes the industrial production of the nation. New England contains Boston, which for over a century was the intellectual center of the country. Often taken together, in this book considered separately, these two regions are characterized by a predominance of industry and production, by a concentration of wealth and control, by policy-forming and idea-germinating activities at all levels, and by the development of techniques for disseminating them.

The South is tobacco country, horse country and, above all, cotton country. It provided us with most of our national leaders in the early days of the Republic and has bequeathed us a legacy of a romantic and gracious way of life of singular appeal in a commercial and technological era. Of late it is becoming more and more an industrial region.

The Midwest is a great fertile farm under which are found layers of coal and other valuable minerals, so that industry is as well developed as agriculture. There are really two Midwests existing side-by-side, the grain-growing, stock-raising, dairying, agricultural Midwest, and a galaxy of industrial cities, many of which are world capitals for their particular products.

The Southwest is a country of mining and stock raising, of vast expanses and colorful history, of guest ranches and cosmopolitan winter resorts. The Central Northwest, with its plains and upland ranges, is the country of stock raising par excellence, the home of the cowboy and

16

the sheep rancher; its great mountains also contain mines, are the locale of national parks and scenic attractions. The Far West is the land of the sun worshippers, with its growing metropolitan areas, its Hollywood, its beaches, its citrus groves; and to the north the land of tall timber, salmon fishing and water power. With an airplane industry and steel plants inherited from war days, the Far West is putting up a battle for industrial independence.

Culturally, too, the regions have their differences. It may accurately be said of America that its literature is regional, crystallizing the regional background and focusing regional aspirations. There is not space here to trace American literary history but, in our own time, think only of Sinclair Lewis's *Main Street,* Steinbeck's *Grapes of Wrath,* Erskine Caldwell's *Tobacco Road,* Margaret Mitchell's *Gone With the Wind,* Louis Bromfield's *The Farm,* Oliver LaFarge's *Laughing Boy,* John Marquand's *The Late George Apley.*

Yet, Beveridge to the contrary, the great regions are united in an essential Americanism. The United States is a league of nations within a nation; however unlike the various sections, the states are still united. "Thou varied charm of different States, yet one identity only," chanted Whitman.

One of the early critics of the American scene was a Frenchman named Jacques who declared that he didn't know whether America was going to perdition or Paradise but that, whichever it was, he knew she would get there first! Speed is one resultant of energy, and speed has been a characteristic of the unfolding of America.

To build up the empire of the Caesars took many centuries. It took a couple of millenniums to bring modern European civilization to maturity. America grew up literally in a few generations. Into the untouched continent went the settlers, wresting it from the Indians, felling trees, breaking the land to plough, farming a thousand acres where their ancestors had farmed ten. They harnessed the rivers, built dams, rendered the desert fertile, dug out the mineral wealth and transformed it. They telescoped the work of a millennium into three centuries; the speed of the achievement was breath-taking.

The curtain went down on the drama of the American frontier in 1890 when the Census Bureau announced that to all intents and purposes the era of "free land" was over. European historians tend to think of American history as colorless, but the history of the Old World has nothing to match the movement of Americans westward unless it be in the treks of the Huns, the Goths, the Mongols or the recent building up of Siberia by the Soviets. Within the confines of a century, millions of emigrants poured into the virtually uninhabited western half of this continent.

The precise significance of the American's telescoping of history can be better appreciated when it is realized that the world has changed more in the last century than in all previous centuries of recorded history. And the United States was a major factor in that change. Agriculture in George Washington's day did not differ essentially from agriculture in the time of Nebuchadnezzar. People still ploughed with horses, oxen or mules. To go places, they went by road, on foot or behind a horse. Suddenly came the industrial revolution. America being the newest and richest country, and enterprise and initiative being American traits, it was in America that most of the inventions were developed, and it was in America that all of them

18

Indian well, New Mexico

were applied to the fullest extent. Here was a new frontier, a new outlet for American energy.

Actually, there have been four "frontiers" in the growth of America. The first — which repeated itself in successive waves — lay in the land itself and the opportunity to open it up, settle it, cause it to prosper. The second was technological — the opportunities created by invention which brought about the age of the machine. The industrial revolution led to the third, the frontier of opportunity to exploit our superabundant natural resources. The fourth — today's frontier — is provided by the rising standard of living, the origination of new industries and the American's innate, creative faith in the future.

In 1856 a man reached St. Paul, Minnesota, a few weeks too late to join the last group of emigrants to leave that year for the Far West. He remained in St. Paul and, with the coming of the era of steam, spanned the Northwest with a network of steel: the Great Northern Railroad. His name was James J. Hill, and his story dramatizes the replacing of one frontier by another. Opportunities provided by the opening up of new land were replaced by opportunities in the development of machinery and the exploitation of natural resources.

In a few decades after the appearance of Deere's steel plow, Hussey's reaper, Peter Cooper's "Tom Thumb" engine that ripped along the tracks of the B. & O. at the staggering speed of eighteen miles an hour, the development of rail and steamship routes, of electricity and the telegraph opened up new regions. The plains of the Central Northwest couldn't have been farmed without windmills, wire and railroads. The railroad, again, coupled the timber of Michigan with the newly developed craft of making furniture by machinery. Gushing oil wells brought towns to life in Pennsylvania, Texas, Oklahoma, California. Here was still another opportunity for enterprise, initiative to invade new territory, take chances and perhaps reap a great reward.

This part of our history provided background for a conflict of Titans — epic characters who grasped at and often seized power and riches. There came the days of Jay Gould, Jim Hill, Commodore Vanderbilt, Collis P. Huntington, the Mackays, the Clarks, the Guggenheims. Behind the procession of names can be discerned traces of involved and far-flung plots, disasters and successes; of ruthless contests on Capitol Hill and in state legislatures. But the accomplishments of men such as these also contained chronicles of planning and realization on a heroic scale.

One unfortunate effect of the opportunity afforded to individuals to exploit great segments of the nation's wealth was that the resources of much of our country were ruthlessly despoiled for private gain without regard to the needs of ordinary settlers seeking to make a living. Thus some great companies deprived farmers on the plains of their water rights; bonanza farms were replaced by the "Dust Bowl"; copper and silver were taken out of the ground as fast as possible; forests were stripped of timber. Hand in hand with enterprise and initiative went rapacity, greed and waste. Nevertheless, there were still new horizons to justify American confidence in an expanding economy.

The first frontiers are no longer with us today, except in the form of new products, new industries which in the normal course of things replace industries that are obsolescent. But the habit of mind formed by the early frontier persists. New conditions imposed their outlook on the man from Europe, ordinarily cautious, restrained, the product of an old civili-

20

South Carolina garden

zation. Of course, those who came to the New World were hardy and brave, willing to take chances and make sacrifices. Few sluggards or weaklings arrived, and they were soon weeded out. That set the tone. Then, as the coastal strip was settled, the more restless, the more adventurous and liberty-loving pushed farther west. As the frontier advanced, the frontier attitude—bold, openhanded, friendly, on the whole optimistic, democratic, hospitable, courteous—became ingrained in our national temperament. The American's underlying philosophy is based on a feeling that everything is progressing toward something better, that there is plenty more of whatever he wants, and that the supply will steadily increase. In virtually none of our manifold activities have we reached static conditions. We are still benefiting by a superabundance of material resources. And, whether the American's innate conviction is true or false, he is still characterized by buoyant optimism and breezy confidence.

More than anyone else, the American believes in the future. From earliest beginnings until the present day, in spite of shocks and vicissitudes which balanced the more exaggerated upswings, despite the impact of wars, the future has always been as real and as vivid in the American mind as the present. Whitman wrote:

> "The Present holds thee not—for such vast growth as thine,
> For such unparallel'd flight as thine,
> The Future only holds thee and can hold thee."

True, the American's confidence is based on the conviction of an expanding market; it relates to things material. In the spiritual realm he is still diffident. Yet there are signs that even here he is beginning to find himself. The trend of the arts is away from European models toward a truly native style. The undeniable beauty of the skyscraper lies in functional design, not in the reproduction of classic motifs. In some of his dwelling houses Frank Lloyd Wright admittedly tried to accent the quiet, level beauty of the prairie. Many objects designed for use, airplanes, radial engines and the like, have an innate beauty of their own. Norman Bel Geddes believes that the "desire and craving for objects of good design is increasing rapidly in the mass of the people." American painting finds its true expression in the work of men like Grant Wood and Thomas Benton rather than in feeble imitations. There is a whole generation of young musicians who were given unusual opportunities during the war. Jazz, universally considered to interpret the temper of the modern age, spread all over the world. It is the gift of the American Negro, with his primitive intensity and natural musical instinct.

And just as artists are turning to their own country for inspiration and better understanding, so the people of the different regions are visiting, studying and understanding other regions.

One of the direct and obvious benefits of the machine has been to provide means of travel by automobile, railroad and passenger plane. If, in the early days of mill, mine and factory, machines made slaves, in the fullness of time they created a new type of freedmen, releasing more people from the bondage of place and enabling them to enjoy spots of historic interest and scenic beauty.

"Know thyself" was a dictum of the ancients. And a better understanding of his own homeland is what the American of today should experience when he sets out to look at America.

22

Wheat field, South Dakota

Look at America

Color and Space

WHEN THE EARTH was shaped, streams of fiery lava forced their way to the surface from the seething core. Aeons passed; glaciers came and went; the volcanic outpourings were fashioned into fantastic forms, sculptured by wind and sand, thrown into relief by chasm-cutting rivers and, because of the presence of minerals, splashed with all the colors of the inferno from which they had come—ochre and vermillion, cinnamon, buff and purple. Parts of the world still suggest the violence and upheaval that took place at the dawn of time. One such region is the American Southwest.

Some sections of it, even today, give the feeling of belonging to an earlier period in the earth's history. There are deep-cleft canyons; granite peaks jabbing the sky; interminable levels of sunken desert scarred by dry arroyos—all drenched in brilliant sunshine; mysterious caverns where stalactites and stalagmites reach ghostly fingers toward each other.

The Southwest is a fitting background for the human pageant that has been played against it: a pageant of cliff-dwellers, of Apache raiders, of glittering conquistadores, of American trappers and forty-niners, sheriffs and gamblers, sheepherders and cowboys, homesteaders and Mormons, cotton tycoons and oil kings, style experts and shipping magnates—types as varied as the stratifications in its own Grand Canyon.

What is the Southwest? Where South meets West, by definition—and with some of the characteristics of both. It is where black land changes to prairie, where oleanders and live oaks give way to sagebrush and mesquite. It is where the Indians had to make room for Spaniards coming up from the South, who in turn had to make room for American pioneers as they rolled the frontier toward the West.

Its confines are not very different today from those roughed out in a series of bold strokes

27

by Spanish explorers and missionaries a century before English settlers set foot on this continent. To the men from Castile the entire region between the Mississippi and the Pacific was merely the northern part of the great colony of New Spain; and, when the Mexicans revolted from the mother country, all that part of it lying north of the Rio Grande was named *Nuevo Mexico*.

The Southwest today includes the whole of Texas, once a sovereign power and still an empire in its own right, with cotton fields, oil wells, lush deltas, great ports and modern cities, as well as tremendous cattle ranges that fling themselves over the horizon. It also includes Oklahoma, a frontier within the memory of its inhabitants—land of oil, wheat, and the Cherokee strip; and, of course, New Mexico and Arizona. Its reaches follow one route of the forty-niners west until the Arizona deserts merge with those of California, and the Sierra Nevadas intercept rain clouds from the Pacific and spill them back in the fertile coastal valleys.

The Southwest's considerably more than half a million square miles offer great variety in landscape, weather, plants and animals. There you can simmer in a desert in winter or shiver on a glacial peak in summer. It is possible to hunt marmots one day and snowshoe rabbits the next. You can descend far below the earth's surface in steep-walled canyons hollowed out by rivers or in mine shafts sunk by man. On the plain, you can set your speedometer needle at sixty and keep it there for hours. Look at Texas: one part of it suggests the languorous Deep South; another, the hustling Middle West; another, the citrus groves of Florida; another, the true Southwest, where you can meet three cultures—Indian, Spanish and American—not only in archaeological remains, but in human beings living side by side. The Southwest is consequently a land of startling incongruities. Wattled wickiups and flat-roofed pueblos jostle modern villas and luxurious hotels. The sunburned man in a wide-brimmed Stetson may be a ranch owner, or he may be a corporation lawyer from Wall Street. The Indian in a blanket may have talked with D. H. Lawrence and Peter Hurd. Debutantes and society matrons mingle with cowpokes and Chinese cooks.

There have been three phases in the history of the Southwest; three empires have held sway. The ancient Indians who looked down from their mesas and were astounded to see knights in armor and plumes come riding through the dust surely did not suspect the end of their dominion. Nor did the descendants of those knights, the rich *haciendados* or great ranch owners, with their feudal retainers in sleepy Spanish villages, suspect from the infiltration of American trappers and scouts in gradually increasing numbers that their bailiwick would in

28

turn be absorbed by the energetic builders of a rich, modern, mineral and agricultural empire.

Mystery surrounds the origins of the first civilizations in the Southwest, but parts of the story can be pieced together from relics and ruins. Caves and holes in the cliffs tell of the Basket Makers, who inhabited northern Arizona and New Mexico hundreds of years before Christ. Broken pots and shell ornaments reveal the culture of the civilized Hohokam—in Pima language, "the people who have gone"—who built networks of irrigating canals. The predecessors of the Hopi built well-laid, symmetrical houses in canyon walls at Mesa Verde and Canyon de Chelly. The ancestors of the Pueblos built a hundred-room skyscraper in Chaco Canyon, containing a series of ceremonial halls, and left fine examples of pottery and inlaid work.

Each of these ancient peoples seems to have laid down its utensils as if for a moment and suddenly vanished, for few burial urns or graves have been found. Their going is one of the great mysteries in the story of the Indian. Maybe they fled the specter of drought. Maybe they fled fierce tribes from the north, such as the Apaches and Comanches, just as Hopi farmers of a later day were driven to build their villages on the tops of inaccessible mesas as a protection against the wandering Navajo and the plundering Spaniard.

So ended the first Southwestern civilization, and in its place came another, spread by followers of the King of Spain. Intrepid and greedy explorers, fanatical missionaries dared heat and thirst, torture and death to bring the sword and the cross to the Southwest. Their story is as colorful as any in history. Cabeza de Vaca, one of the few survivors of a cavalcade of mounted knights who came to grief in the jungles of Florida, slew and ate his horses, made a boat of the skins, was wrecked on the (now Texan) shores of the Gulf, spent six years as a captive of the Indians, was freed and wandered overland to Mexico City. In all he traveled some six thousand miles, passing through the site of San Antonio and, according to some reports, building a village where El Paso now stands. The black-skinned Estevan, who accompanied De Vaca, met his death at the hands of the Zunis when he dressed in rattles, gourds and feathers to make them think he was a god—but he is the only Negro explorer of North America to win undying fame. Don Francisco Vasquez de Coronado, with his knights in burnished armor, his caparisoned horses, his herds and his flocks—for it was the Spaniard who gave the Indian his horse and the Southwest its cattle—pushed to the walls of the Grand Canyon itself, swung eastward through what is now New Mexico, up through the panhandles of Texas and Oklahoma, into Kansas and maybe even as far as Nebraska. Coronado was seeking the Seven Cities

29

of Cibola, whose streets, so the whisper ran, were paved with gold, and whose lintels were studded with turquoise. Disillusionment was his only reward. The wealth of the Southwest remained undisturbed, to be discovered and exploited centuries later by others, including the descendants of Spain's hereditary enemy, the English. And it took other forms than gold.

For there came a time when the violent Apaches began to see other faces than those of Spanish warriors, padres and ranch owners. Hunters, Indian-fighters, trappers and guides filtered into the region—the prototype of them all being New Mexico's renowned Kit Carson. It was not long before ox and mule teams from Missouri established a trail to the ancient capital of Santa Fe, bringing Yankee firearms, hardware and yard goods in exchange for furs, silver and gold from the local mines and for rawhide bags full of shiny silver dollars from old Mexico. With the discovery of gold in California the trickle of pioneers broadened into a stream. At passes and junctions, towns were born. Grubstake prospectors dropped off to try their luck in juniper-dotted canyons. With the finding of copper and the development of the cattle industry came the railroad, threading its way along the Santa Fe trail, and the Southwest as we know it was born—a realm of ranches that stretch farther than you can see on a clear day (and most days are clear); terrace upon terrace of copper-bearing quartzite baking in the sun; giant dams that repeat a thousandfold the Indian trick of transforming the desert into a garden.

This new Southwest has not displaced the old. In Oklahoma, oil-enriched Indians wear diamonds in their ears—a sight that would surely have been gratifying to Coronado. Custer's old Indian scout was still alive in 1946. Oklahoma (whose name in Choctaw means "Red People"), given to the Five Civilized Tribes in 1830, was bought back, settled, and was graduated to statehood in 1907. As a state it is older than Arizona and New Mexico, which joined the Union in 1912, but there are many Oklahomans alive who can remember when it was thrown open to the white man. Twenty thousand settlers raced into the Cherokee strip, hell for leather. All they wanted was homesteads, but in due course black wealth was to gush out of the earth, making Tulsa the "oil capital of the world." There are derricks on the lawn of the State Capitol at Oklahoma City.

Texas' story is more complex. Yielding more oil than Oklahoma, and some 40 per cent of all U.S. production, the Lone Star State also leads in production of cotton, natural gas, beef cattle, sheep and goats, sulfur and turkeys. Indeed Texas is so big that it is no surprise at all to find many areas that are not in the least typical of the Southwest. Broadly, the state

30

is bisected by the Balcones Fault, a fracture in the earth's crust which starts northwest of Austin and swings down just west of San Antonio to reach the Mexican border at Del Rio. The region lying to the east of it, with piney woods, black lands and rice paddies, white and Negro share-croppers, hibiscus and live oaks, looks nostalgically back at the Old South. Here you will find the cotton capitals, zooming Houston, already one of the busiest ports in the country, and sophisticated Dallas, where you can hear the Metropolitan Opera and see fashion shows rivaling those of New York. Both cities pride themselves on their symphony orchestras. Down the coast is the delta of the Rio Grande, with grapefruit, orange and lemon groves, palms and palmettos, resembling nothing so much as a slice of Florida.

The size of Texas, again, makes it easy to understand how a generous portion of it belongs to the real Southwest. El Paso, for instance, is actually nearer the Pacific Coast than to the Gulf of Mexico—and more closely linked with the mines and ranches of New Mexico and Arizona than with the Pecos region of Texas east of it. The saying goes that you know you are in the Southwest when you get a first sniff of high, dry air. But long before you reach the high country, as you move west from the Balcones Fault, plateau, plain and prairie are dotted with mesquite, which gives way to low sagebrush, Spanish bayonet, greasewood and cactus.

The Southwest really begins at San Antonio, where the flavor of Spanish colonial days is as strong as the pimento in an *arroz con pollo.* Here the Franciscan padres, radiating out from the old mission that became immortal as the Alamo, brought faith and practical guidance to Indian neophytes. In the next phase, the city was the starting point of the old Chisholm Trail, along which thousands of steers were driven each year to railheads in distant Kansas. It became the capital of the cow country, where the ranches are still as big as any in the world, the land of the open range where cattle wandered at will, where American "knights of the saddle" vied in daring with their predecessors, the knights of Coronado. Farther west, El Paso, the "Pass to the North" of Spaniard and Mexican, was the gateway to the West, not only for explorers like Cabeza de Vaca, Onate and Espejo, but for trappers and traders, forty-niners and prospectors, homesteaders and Confederate veterans, and finally for the railroads. Through it Texas ranchers pushed west along the extension of the Great Plains and the southern slopes of the Rockies to mingle with silver miners and sheepherders in the development of a new state, New Mexico.

But silver and gold, cattle and sheep were not to be the most significant features of the life of New Mexico. For centuries the ancient city of Santa Fe was the capital of the whole

31

Southwest. Culturally it still is. Its atmosphere suggests the Old World; a bell in one of its churches, brought from Spain by caravel and from Mexico City by ox-cart, bears the date 1356. Around Santa Fe, more than in any other area, the three cultures mingle without losing their identity. Indians grinding corn on their mesas, Spanish-Americans prodding burros along the sun-baked plazas of somnolent villages, American painters and writers working and theorizing in sequestered retreats are free to live their own lives. This juxtaposition of strains makes for picturesqueness, as do the mountains rolling down to fawn-colored plains interspersed with feathery groves of willow and cottonwood. The region draws thousands of visitors, some to nurse their way back to health in the dry air, some to visit the national parks and monuments and natural wonders such as the Carlsbad Caverns and Ship Rock, some to watch the Indian dances, and all to bask in a grateful sun. "Dude wrangling," as the cowboys call looking after visitors, is one of the state's major industries.

No less attractive is Arizona. Perhaps nowhere in the world has Nature created a more imposing monument than the Grand Canyon. In the Rainbow Natural Bridge and the Painted Desert the naturally violent colors of the Southwestern landscape are intensified; in the Petrified Forest are tree trunks a million years old. The cities of Phoenix, in the center of the state, and Tucson, in the more arid south, are so crowded with visitors from other parts of the country, especially in winter, that they have the cosmopolitan atmosphere of Santa Fe.

Yet the traveler does not drive ten miles inside Arizona without realizing there is an industry even more important than guest-ranching. Spark-filled smoke from great smelters is evidence that much of the copper produced in the United States is taken from the state's canyoned slopes. Hill towns have seen claims that changed hands for a few thousand dollars produce hundreds of millions of dollars' worth of copper. Some of the towns became bywords for lawlessness and violence of the old frontier days before relapsing into ghost towns or settling down to comfort and respectability.

So much for the miner; the farmer found wealth in another way. After scratching a soil that was parched most of the year, then drenched when the rains finally came, he turned to irrigation. Why not copy the ancient Hohokams and build canals? Why not store up life-giving waters? Today Roosevelt Dam and other great engineering projects have transformed thousands of acres. In the middle of the desert the motorist abruptly meets serried rows of lettuce and cantaloupe, citrus trees and date palms. He might with some reason wonder whether he had

32

reached the Pacific Coast. Yet, only a few miles farther west, sun and sand regain their sway—here the desert is so blistering and arid that not even the most miserable rat can survive.

The Southwest is fabulous. Its landscape defies traditional concepts. Even the flora is weird. Giant saguaros raise their arms like overblown candelabra; the ocotillo spreads its wand-like branches. Silvery cottonwoods full of chattering blackbirds cluster about the river beds. Scrub oak, piñon and juniper straggle up the foothills to blend into forests of yellow pine. And the animals themselves seem somehow unreal: in addition to the ubiquitous coyote and prairie dog, there are such creatures as the Gila monster, the rattlesnake, the tarantula.

The scale of this land had its effect on the men who lived there. So did the fact that much of it is a dry, difficult country to work. With the exception of the northern woods and the oases created by irrigation, there is nothing intimate about the Southwestern landscape. It is hard and prickly, like a cactus—armed to withstand man's efforts to master it. The men who tamed this wild region had to be tough in fibre. They could be courteous—when a real or fancied insult meant blood on the barroom floor. They could be chivalrous—in a country where the few women brave enough to inhabit it needed protection from Apaches, mountain wolves and desperadoes. They could be hospitable—when the next ranch was a hundred miles away.

A worthy descendant of these frontiersmen is the typical Southwesterner of today. Chances are he is tall, hard and well built. And he has a largeness of spirit as well as of body, induced by living in a setting where man is insignificant. To the newcomer he will apply his own standards. With the Southwesterner, the firmness of your character counts more than your income. He is openhearted and openhanded. The visitor from other parts, the Eastern city-dweller, the Middle Western business man, the prairie farmer, gains by familiarity with the Southwest. There is little inclination for detail, for minor worries and flurries of spirit, in a region where the horizon is a hundred miles away, where the high dry air is frosty in the morning and baked yellow by noon, where the lurid colors of the landscape shock the imagination. There the sky is cobalt by day, ultramarine velvet at night, and the atmosphere so clear you think you can reach out and pluck the stars.

33

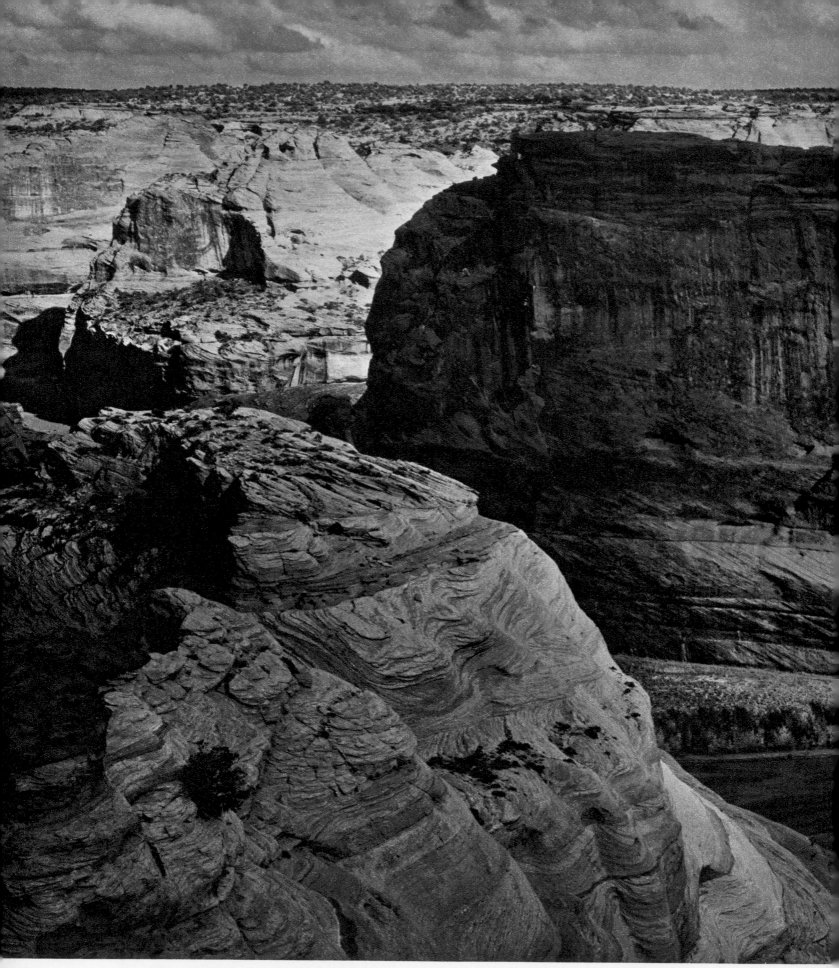

The color and space of the Southwest are perhaps nowhere better portrayed than in this massive gorge in northeastern Arizona — the Canyon de Chelly — whose red sandstone walls rise to heights of 1,000 feet and wind for miles along an ancient river course. Here, centuries ago, lived the cliff dwellers, who farmed flat bottom lands, climbed to their homes at night and

pulled ladders up after them to be safe from attack. Nearly 150 cliff dwellings, well preserved today, were left by this vanished race. To the Navajo, who later inhabited the Canyon but not its cliffs, the towering walls proved more a trap than a protection. Kit Carson's Indian fighters marched over river ice in the winter of 1863 and captured 7,000 of them.

35

The White House, so named because white clay was used in its construction, is one of the largest and best preserved of Canyon de Chelly cliff dwellings. Originally four stories high, the structure has walls of carefully laid stone, aligned so truly that even today they seem to have been built with the aid of a plumb line. It was occupied between 1050 and 1300 A.D.

Showpiece of Southwest vegetation, the saguaro cactus takes 100 years to grow its full 50 feet.

A well-known feature of Indian life in the Southwest is the Hopi snake dance, performed with live snakes in the villages of northern Arizona. It is the climactic phase, and the only one open to public view, of a nine-day Hopi ritual in supplication for rain. Despite inroads by white civilization, Indians of this region retain much of their ancient customs and character.

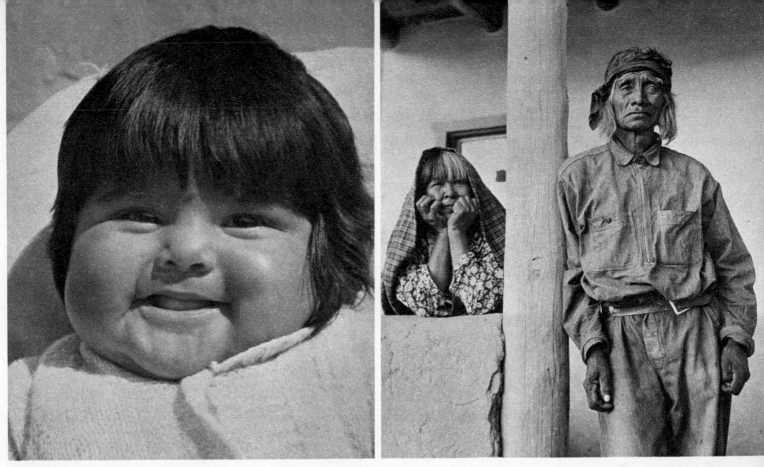

The young and the old personify the vigor and the wisdom of the Southwest's Indian tribes.

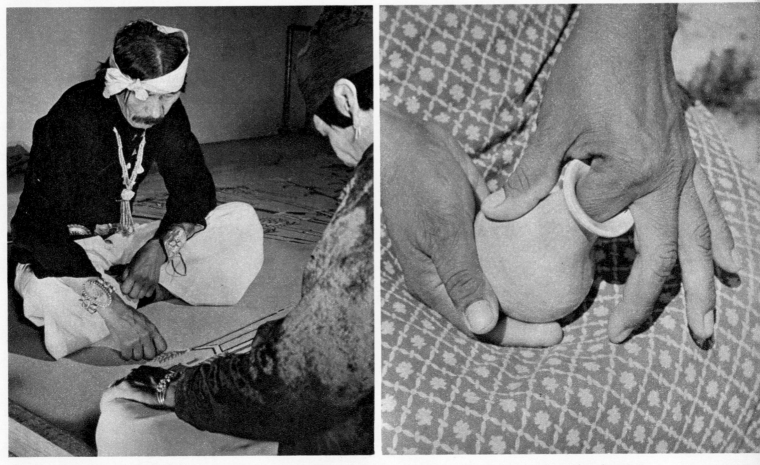

With varicolored sand and minerals, "sand painters" or shamans of the Navajo tribe fashion symbolic figures used in votive and healing ceremonies. Begun at dawn, the "paintings" are swept away again at dusk. This extraordinary art is rivaled by the pottery making (right) of the Pueblos, who learn from infancy to work with clay, produce ware of delicate symmetry.

The night-blooming cereus, shown here in full midnight splendor, is one of 100 varieties of cactus and of more than 6,000 species of plant life that flourish in the Southwest.

Skiing through green mountain woods is not uncommon in the Southwest's regions of late spring snows. The most popular ski courses are near Santa Fe, New Mexico, and Flagstaff, Arizona.

41

A cowboy astride a high-bucking steer rocketing from the bullpen into the ring keynotes the thrills of a Southwest rodeo, one of many such riding and roping exhibitions held in the region each year. Outgrowth of informal sessions when cowboys showed off their skill to each other, rodeos are as much a part of Southwest life as is baseball in the nation as a whole.

JOHN HEATH
TAKEN FROM
County Jail &
LYNCHED
By Bisbee Mob
IN TOMBSTONE
Feb. 22ᵈ 1884

DAN DOWD
RED SAMPLE
TEX HOWARD
BILL DeLANEY
DAN KELLY

LEGALLY
HANGED
~~MARCH 18 88th~~
1884

Graves of bad men hanged legally and otherwise — like these in Tombstone, Arizona — stir memories of the legendary struggles with lawlessness that color the Southwest's history. The hanging of cattle rustlers, killers and other outlaws in the early days of the cattle country was often a community affair, with little regard for the formalities of justice.

The moon over Hernandez, New Mexico, illumines a scene familiar throughout the Southwest
— the little village sleeping peacefully behind the graves of its founders, the semi-arid terrain

44

stretching away toward mountains in the distance, and the simply designed church. Distances are deceptive in this region — the mountains are at least 15 miles beyond the town.

The enchanted Mesa near Acoma, shunned by the Indians through belief it is haunted, is typical nonetheless of the rocky heights on which many Pueblo communities in New Mexico were built.

Atop Acoma Rock, almost as high and precipitous as the Enchanted Mesa, Pueblo Indians dwell in adobe homes as they did when Coronado's army discovered the community in 1540. The date of its founding unknown, Acoma is perhaps the oldest continuously inhabited place in America.

The stone rather than adobe walls (left) of the Spanish Mission at Quari, New Mexico, and the Spanish-designed oven at Taos were built by the Indians after the arrival of the conquerors.

47

This "ghost ranch" region of the Chama Valley in New Mexico, where erosion by wind and rain destroyed vegetation that once fed cattle on its slopes, emphasizes the harsh terms set by

nature in the Southwest for those who seek a livelihood from the land. Vast areas are arid or semi-arid and irrigation, begun centuries ago by the Indians, today is a major concern.

49

North of Santa Fe, in Ranchos de Taos (one of three sister villages called simply Taos), is Saint Francis of Assisi Mission, perhaps the best known of New Mexico's churches.

50

At nearby Taos Pueblo, Indians perform the Buffalo Dance each Christmas season to insure good hunting, wear horned and shaggy headdresses (left), are lured to the hunters by a sole woman dancer. The Crown Dance (headdress at right) was originally enacted by Apaches only in times of tribal crises such as war and epidemics, now marks an annual Fourth of July fiesta at the Mescalero Indian Reservation in southern New Mexico.

Santa Fe is at its gayest each Labor Day week end when a three-day fiesta, inaugurated in 1712, commemorates the Spaniard De Vargas' reconquest of New Mexico from the Indians in 1692. Traditional start of the festival is the burning of Zozobra (above), symbol of gloom; from the first flare of fire the city bursts into holiday enthusiasm marked by street dancing, Indian tribal dancing and parades.

Three phases of the Southwest's topography — a pattern of strange and ageless contrasts —
are brought together in this view of the Guadalupe Mountains in the Lincoln National Forest
of southeastern New Mexico. The yucca plant in the foreground flourishes oddly in the dusty,
sparsely vegetated soil common to the Southwest's arid regions. Beyond this lie salt flats —

52

incredibly level stretches of salt and nothing else. Farther on rise the tortured slopes and rugged cliffs of the mountains. In the more than half a million square miles that comprise the Southwest region, such scenes are common, with baked desert plains within a few hours ride of snowbound peaks; lush jungle-like bayous a few miles from bone-dry arroyos.

River scenes in Texas contrast sharply. This is a view, at a low-water period, of the Brazos, a major flood problem of the Southwest. It flows from the Panhandle to the Gulf of Mexico.

Some 50 miles from the Brazos, a bayou of the Neches River near Beaumont, with Spanish moss hanging from swampland trees, provides a setting for fishing in semitropical solitude.

Showplace of the Southwest's cattle country is the King Ranch, whose cowboys are shown here driving a herd to water. So big that autos crossing pastures carry compasses, the ranch sprawls over a million and a quarter acres of southern Texas; has its own stores, schools and churches, breeds its own pigs, sheep and fine horses. King Ranch also has its special breed of cattle, combining heat resistance of the India Brahma with U. S. shorthorn beef quality.

56

A King Ranch cowhand ropes a young heifer for branding. The ranch boasts "the world's best cowboys," Mexican-Americans who hand down riding and roping skill to sons and grandsons.

The horse is the friend and indispensable helper of the Texas cattleman. Here a young herd lopes through a valley on the King Ranch, where they are raised and trained for the range.

Framed between spherical storage tanks, this superfractionating unit of a refinery at Baytown, Texas, symbolizes the development of the Southwest's greatest source of wealth — oil. Super-fraction is a process for separating high and low octanes in naphthas produced by "cracking"

58

operations, was developed at Baytown to increase the output of aviation gasoline. Major producers of petroleum products in the Southwest are Oklahoma and Texas, with Texas fields and refineries accounting for approximately 40 per cent of the nation's total output.

59

This is the entrance to the historic Alamo in San Antonio, perhaps the most famous of Texas shrines. Here in 1836, during the struggle that resulted eventually in independence, at least 185 Texas patriots died in a vain attempt to repulse Mexican forces. The little low gray chapel and ivy-covered walls are all that remain today of the original mission.

Founded in 1720, San Jose Mission, also at San Antonio, was once "queen of the missions" of New Spain. Today its chapel, cloisters, granary and mill are either preserved or restored.

Broad fields of grain gathered into shocks attest that oil-rich Oklahoma is also an important agricultural state. Leading the nation in the production of alfalfa and broomcorn, Oklahoma also ranks high as a grower of wheat, cotton, corn, oats, spinach and watermelons.

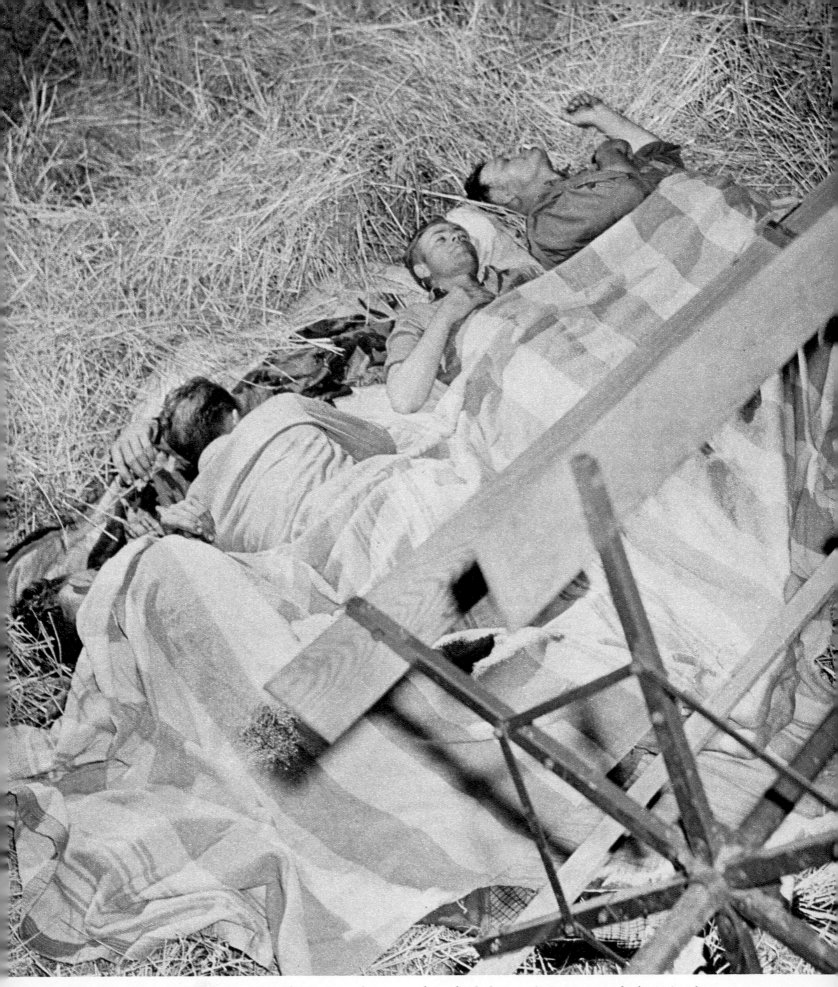

During the wheat harvest in Oklahoma, farm workers bed down their crop and sleep in the open beneath the blades of a reaper. Oklahoma has held second place among the states as a producer of wheat, but its principal yield is in pasture grasses for its livestock industry.

The skyscraper office buildings of Tulsa, which house oil-financing operations second only to New York's, loom beyond storage tanks and refining installations that bespeak Tulsa's position as "the oil capital of the world." Oklahoma's second largest city, situated on the Arkansas River, Tulsa thrives as well on industries allied to petroleum, with many machine shops, tank companies, rig and derrick manufacturers and the like. To Osage Indians and other land-

owners near Tulsa, the accident of the discovery of oil on their property brought fabulous wealth in the early part of the century. Cheap fuel and abundant sources of raw materials have led to the development of several glass factories, a large cotton mill, chemical works, a furniture factory, steel works and other industrial enterprises. The city is also the commercial and supply center for a rich farming and fruit growing area to the south.

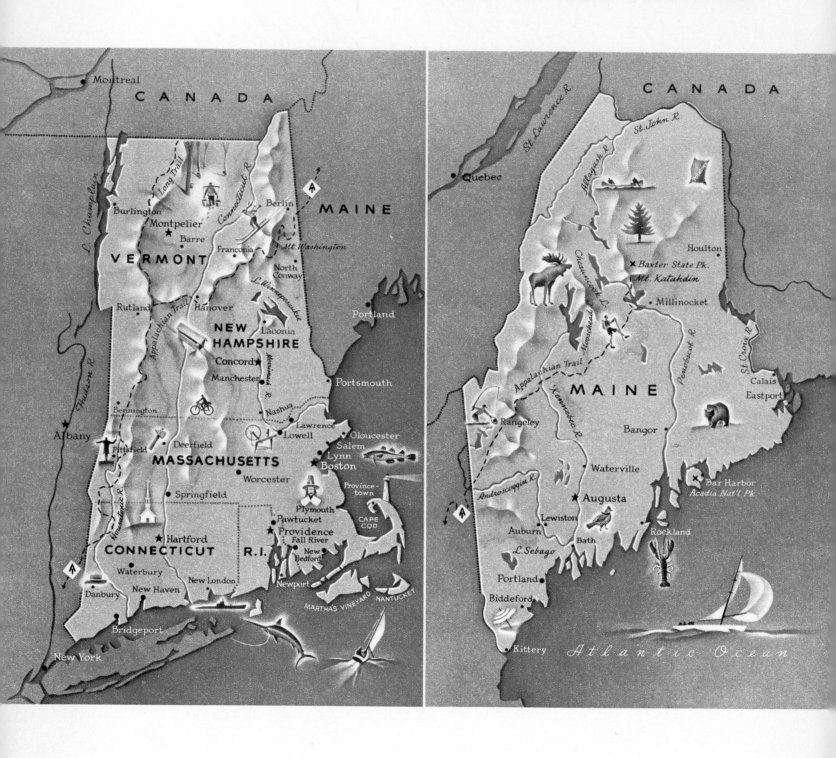

Trade and Tradition

FOR THOSE who would know New England there is a message in the surf-battered ledges and crags of its rocky coast, in dark islands, in barren stretches of shifting dunes and salt marshes, in glacier-moulded hillocks and knolls, boulder-strewn fields, in stone walls and twisted apple trees.

The message is not always easy to read, particularly when forbidding cliffs are balanced by gentle, tide-washed inlets; when the boldness of a headland jutting from the sea is softened by a mantle of pines; when, in October, the woods are brushed with crimson and gold. But it is there, nonetheless. And it helps explain New England.

The essence of New England is strength of character. A rugged land proved the nurturing ground for a rugged breed of men. Pilgrim and Puritan; trapper, hunter, and fisherman; dogmatist and dissenter; trader and merchant; skipper and pirate; zealot, patriot and founding father were distinguished alike by that firmness of resolve that goes by the name of character. And truly men would have to be as hard as granite boulders, as tough as hickory nuts, and quite possibly as wry as crab apples to leave — as those who settled New England did — the comforts of a civilized land for the sake of independence of thought; to brave the ocean in frail vessels and wrest a living from the wilderness; to win liberty by fighting for it and help found a new nation; to send men, machines and money throughout a continent.

The essence of New England is character — molded by geography. Pushing back the forest and making a living from a recalcitrant soil threw the early settler on his own resources, sharpened his natural self-reliance. He learned to keep his own counsel, do his own thinking. Obliged to make every penny count, he became frugal. He also became a shrewd trader — which was to have its effect on the economic life of the nation. Unimpressed by the notions and

67

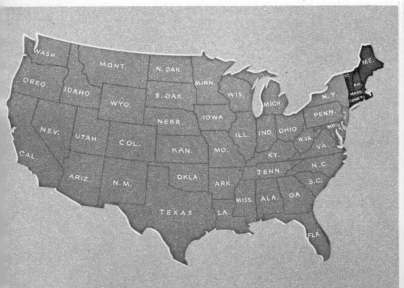

pretensions of outsiders, he didn't go in for show. Thus he resembled the old houses in Boston's aristocratic Back Bay, which are unassuming as well as dignified. The Yankee has a homespun integrity; in temperament he is more akin to the Scot than any other race. They say it is the stones in the orchards that give the peculiar flavor to New England apples. Its inhabitants have the same flavor — juicy and wholesome, but a trifle astringent. They are sharp as the climate, rugged as the landscape.

And because they are, New Englanders have been quick to grasp leadership, whether in a war for independence, in commerce and industry, in settling a new nation or in establishing the foundations of its culture.

The men who forsook their placid English farm land for the right to worship as they saw fit were not loath to dump the hated English tea into Boston Harbor; to die on the cobbles of State Street in the Boston Massacre; to stand up to the Redcoats on the village green at Lexington, and stem the British onslaught at Bunker Hill. And New England guided much of the political thinking of the fledgling republic. Many of the ideas later embodied in the Bill of Rights slumbered two years in the Charter Oak at Hartford.

Just as New Englanders seized on the oppressions of George III to turn them into independence, so also they turned early to a natural advantage to grasp commercial leadership. New England's hills sloped eastward to the sea, and eastward and southward her streams flowed into it. She had hundreds of natural harbors and plenty of the tallest and straightest spruce and oak for masts and ship timbers. And so New Englanders became seafarers, as the "sacred" codfish hanging in the State House in Boston mutely testifies. Graceful fishing boats put out of Gloucester for the Newfoundland Banks, returning laden with cod and halibut; sturdy whalers from Nantucket scoured the antarctic. Schooners —a product of Yankee ingenuity — carried turpentine, pitch, dried cod and pickled mackerel to the Antilles and brought back brown mahogany, brown rum, and black men for slaves. White-winged clippers, the most graceful and the fleetest sailing vessels in the world, left Boston Harbor, rounding the Horn to the Orient and returning with tea and silk. Chinese could be heard along the streets of old Salem, and Indian potentates who had never heard of the United States thought the little tea capital was a country in its own right.

In a crisis, moreover, masters of ships were not reluctant to mount cannon along the gunwales of their vessels and give the Royal Navy as good as they got, ship for ship, in stinging

68

rounds of grape. Often they were victorious and returned rich prizes to New England ports.

It wasn't always smooth sailing, however, for Yankee skippers. When ships began to be built of iron instead of wood, other sections of the country were in a position to compete on the water. But Yankee resourcefulness reasserted itself. Streams were set to work turning factory wheels — which gave rise to another supremacy. Great manufacturing centers grew up in such communities as Lawrence, Lowell and Fall River in Massachusetts, Pawtucket in Rhode Island, producing machinery and shoes for the Midwest, textiles for the South.

Industrial leadership resulted in yet another form of regional export — and thereby hangs a paradox. The niggardliness of nature had taught the Yankee a certain penuriousness — he had to skimp and save. In the end, this could have only one result: he found himself with an accumulation of savings and in a position to export capital. Even when he prospered he saved his money, and the money went into banks; from the banks it went out to build factories in other sections, to pay for harvesting crops in the grain country, develop mines in the mountain areas, build cities in the West and railroads everywhere.

In addition to hard cash, New Englanders exported something less tangible. Many were the sons who left New England as their fathers had left Britain, and pushed still farther to the west, establishing frontier after frontier. Men who began by going from door to door with packs on their backs built railroad and mineral empires in the West. In Ohio today you will see village greens surrounded by trim white houses, reflecting cherished recollections of Connecticut or Vermont. For, as the saying goes, "Hard living begets a love of the hard land," and the Yankee is distinguished by a loyalty to his own province so strong as sometimes to give the impression — just as in the case of the English — of a conviction of superiority.

Wherever he went, the Yankee emigrant spread the germs of his own peculiar brand of Anglo-Saxon culture. Thus he affected the course of the nation's growth and the character of its civilization. If the Yankee had not wearied of his backbreaking labors; if, like the Southerner, he could have remained comfortably secure in his acres and in the slaves who tended them, he might not have ventured so far afield. In which case our cultural associations would not have been predominantly those of New England, and Plymouth Rock might not be the symbol of the colonizing of North America by the English.

New Englanders were accustomed to doing their own thinking and as a rule to thinking hard and straight. They did not recoil from problems involving brain work. It was appropriate

69

that Boston should become the center of the intellectual life of the nation. Always to the fore in promoting communal activities, the "Athens of America" built the first public school in the country and founded the first college, dedicated to the memory of John Harvard. The first law school was started in Connecticut. New England produced independent-minded political thinkers like John Adams, Wendell Phillips and William Lloyd Garrison, philosophers like Emerson and Thoreau, jurists like Daniel Webster and Rufus Choate; and almost all of the country's first-line nineteenth-century authors — Longfellow, Hawthorne, Whittier, Henry James. Even today it owns to a majority of the names in *Who's Who in America.* And most of the best-known colleges and private schools are still to be found beside its elm-shaded greens.

The twentieth century brought one more major economic crisis to test the resourcefulness of the Yankee. In the nineteen twenties and thirties industrial leadership which had taken the place of maritime supremacy in the economic life of the region collapsed with a thud. Factories moved away — south — west — anywhere. Unemployment emptied streets of mill towns which became ghost towns almost overnight.

Again the New Englander's enterprise found a solution—by switching from quantity to quality, by reverting even in the factory to the tradition of skilled artisanship in which the area had always been a leader. A renascence took place. With only 6.7 per cent of the population of the country, New England today turns out 10 per cent of the total value added to raw materials by processing. It produces much of the country's finest textiles, food products, books, hats, clocks, airplane engines and propellers, firearms, business machines, sewing machines, hardware, silverware, bells, copper and brass products. In 1940 New England produced more than 60 per cent of the fine cotton goods turned out in this country. A little hill town in Vermont, Springfield, sends machine tools all over the world. Manufactures in the Boston area alone total three billion dollars annually. With all these factories coming, going and being regenerated, it is not surprising that the descendants of the pioneers who came over in the *Mayflower* became outnumbered by immigrants who came over in the steerage. The 1840 potato famine in Ireland began an influx that brought millions of Irish tenant farmers and laborers. So many settled in Boston that it became an Irish city, with the Boston Irish referring to themselves jocularly as the "poor, downtrodden majority." And as the Church plays a vital role in the Irishman's existence, Boston, the home of the Puritan meeting house, the Unitarian Church and the *Christian Science Monitor,* is now predominantly Roman Catholic.

70

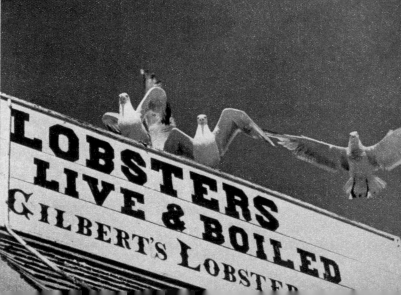

To thousands of others in politically oppressed Europe, the call of liberty and opportunity also proved irresistible. Boston alone now has nearly a quarter million foreign-born Italians, Jews, Poles, Swedes, Germans, Lithuanians and Greeks. More French than English is spoken in many mill towns, and a Polish colony grew up in Salem at the door of Hawthorne's House of Seven Gables. The Portuguese fishermen on the Cape, who came in early from the Azores, still wear colorful costumes in cranberry time and have not forgotten the songs of their country. Today the section has as high a percentage of foreign born as any in the country, yet the Wienawskis and the Nikapouloses and the Angelottis have been assimilated, and the traditional New England atmosphere predominates—except perhaps in the slums of mill towns and large cities—in the mingling of cultures.

The region that during the first half of the nation's existence virtually built up half a continent and furnished its intellectual and cultural leadership is relatively small in size. With an area of some 67,000 square miles, a scant 2 per cent of the national total, all of New England's states could be packed into Missouri and there would still be room for a third of New Jersey. The entire region is roughly half the size of California, a quarter the size of Texas. Yet at one end, in Connecticut, you can almost see the Empire State Building, while at the other, where northern Maine thrusts a salient well into Canada, you are up under the northern lights, hundreds of miles beyond Quebec.

Of New England's eight million population, no less than four fifths live in Connecticut, Massachusetts and Rhode Island, which together represent only two ninths of the total area. Tiny Rhode Island has the startling population density of 627 to the square mile as contrasted with only 25.5 in Maine.

In the three states forming the southern tier of the region the living is easiest and most convenient, yet the rugged—and by the same token sparsely settled—regions are not far away. From yellow beaches to rolling green mountains is often no more than an afternoon's drive. From valleys where graceful white villages succeed each other at frequent intervals it is not far to the great northern forests where moose, bear and lynx are seldom disturbed by man.

Such contrast, especially of mountain and valley, creates great beauty. The independent spirit of its citizens has won for New England the sobriquet of "Switzerland of America," but it has other elements in common with the little Alpine republic—not the least being its scenery. New England's lengthy coast, often forbidding, has sections whose hazy blue-green shore lines

71

suggest the Bay of Naples, and where the little villages have Italian names. Elsewhere the cliffs are reminiscent of English Devon and Cornwall, or the Scottish isles. There is contrast between Cape Cod, the "bare and bended arm of Massachusetts," as Thoreau called it, with its miles of yellow beaches, its dunes, its cranberry bogs, its scrub-pine-covered knolls, and salt marshes along Massachusetts' North Shore, where seagulls perch on the tombstones; between weatherworn grey shingles of Nantucket cottages and the maple clumps, unpainted sugarhouses and redolent sawmills of Vermont.

The charm of New England is intimate. It lies in brooks gurgling around boulders, trout pools dozing beneath arched elms, wharves webbed with nets smelling of seaweed where lobster pots dry in the sun, smacks idling home into quiet coves at sundown. It is to be found in a pre-Revolutionary salt-box house looking out on a shaded lawn, or an old-time fireplace with its iron pothooks, its settle, its copper kettles and brass warming pan. Here it is an elm-shaded street, there a white church with its delicate spire.

In New England you feel the hand of time. It is the most finished part of the country. Even in thriving cities you unexpectedly come on some dignified old house or a crooked cobbled street originally traced by a vagrant cow. The place has the air of having been lived in a long time. It looks and feels settled. There is no excess, no blatancy. It does not claim the highest mountains, the deepest canyon, the biggest dam. You have to look for evidences of newness, rawness, or anything temporary or flimsy, for what is experimental and for what is in bad taste.

It is not surprising, then, that visitors throng to New England in such numbers that in summer the population of some regions is doubled. When they depart each year they leave behind half a billion dollars in the pockets of the sagacious Yankees, who carefully tend their ancestral shrines, teach traffic policemen forbearance, and have set aside more areas for monuments and parks than have any other of the older sections of the country.

The goal of these visitors may be the Vermont hills or sunny harbors and sea-girt headlands of the Maine coast. It may be they come to hunt moose with a camera, to cast for brook trout, to sail eighteen-footers, to put their daughters in camp, to swoop down ski trails or sit back and listen to symphony concerts, according to the season.

Yet it may also be something more. A great many of these visitors are returning to what they think of as home. Some quaint old slate headstone in a hillside cemetery announces that the bones reposing beneath those shady elms belonged to the great-grandparents of the visitor

72

from Dorchester, South Carolina, or Quincy, Illinois. Here is the white-steepled church to which they walked regularly of a Sabbath morning after six days of toil. And this quiet village was once a small settlement where the first colonists to bring the family name to the New World fought off the Indians and wrested a living from the harsh land.

Almost from the moment the visitor crosses the boundary he is surrounded by beauty. And it is not long before he finds the other element he is so often seeking, perhaps unconsciously — the thing he was not able to take with him to West Virginia or Idaho or wherever he settled down. He is finding his past.

There could be no better guide for an intelligent tour of New England than a sense of the past. The thread of that past can be followed, for example, in homes where lived struggling pioneer and prosperous merchant — in rude garrison houses, rambling frame buildings with floors on different levels and oddly assorted windows; in eighteenth-century houses with Georgian ornamentation displayed in pilasters, scrolls, swans' necks, and graceful fanlights over old doorways.

The visitor with one day to spend in New England might best capture the region's spirit by spending a morning in a quiet village like Concord, Old Lyme, or Litchfield; an afternoon in a port like Marblehead, Gloucester, New Bedford, Provincetown or Nantucket — remembering that the first New England whaling ship crossed the equator on the very day the Minutemen took their stand on the green at Lexington. By the wharves one can still savor the good strong smell of brine and tar and oil and the wind blowing in from the sea, can still hear carpenter's hammer and caulker's mallet and, with a little imagination, the rousing chanteys of the mariners of a bygone era. The town meetinghouse with its simplicity, restraint and charm symbolizes all that is best in the New England tradition; the old harbor stands for all that is enterprising and colorful in New England's trade.

73

Since John Cabot edged his ships among its islands in 1498, the spray-worn coast of Maine has been a challenge to mariners, a delight to all who love the sea. Carved by a glacial ice sheet and skirting hundreds of inlets, coves, bays and harbors, the state's water line of more than 2,400 miles winds along a direct shore line of less than 250 miles. From Eastport, with its 25-foot

74

tide range, to the New Hampshire border, the Maine coast is inhabited by a breed of people noted for self-sufficiency and shrewd honesty. Some cultivate tight little farms, but most, in one way or another, are seafarers. Shipbuilding is a major industry, and more than 70,000 residents of Maine draw income directly or indirectly from the state's commercial fisheries.

Lighthouses such as this guide mariners off the Maine coast past rock and reef to safety despite gales which leave their mark on wind-tortured trees.

Maine lobstermen paint their buoys with the care appropriate to a means of livelihood. The floating markers are then attached by ropes to lobster traps which are hauled in daily.

Cultivating potato fields in Aroostook county is the first step in the annual farming cycle that each year since 1924 has given Maine first place in the nation in total potato production.

78

Mt. Katahdin, 5,268 feet high, is one of ten mountains in Maine whose altitudes exceed 4,000 feet. It is the first spot in the United States touched by the rays of the rising sun.

The Minuteman Statue at Lexington, Massachusetts, marks the "birthplace of American liberty" where on April 19, 1775, patriots gave their lives in the first skirmish of the Revolution.

The Old Granary Burying Ground, surrounded by Boston's business district, is the resting place of John Hancock, Samuel Adams and Robert Treat Paine, signers of the Declaration of Independence. Here too are buried Paul Revere, who rode to warn Lexington's Minutemen against the British; Peter Faneuil, who gave Faneuil Hall to the city; the parents of Benjamin Franklin; the victims of the Boston Massacre, and nine governors of Massachusetts.

The sea captain's home — this one on Martha's Vineyard — with roof-top "widow's walk" for sighting ships, and the old powder house at Marblehead are familiar Massachusetts sights.

The informality of wharf houses at Rockport, a popular seaside center for artists, and the stateliness of homes on Boston's Beacon Street are equally characteristic of the state.

Among the mementoes of Massachusetts' seafaring greatness are the figureheads of her clipper ships, which have been preserved in many a museum and private home. In the eighteenth and nineteenth centuries figures like this traveled to the world's ports on New England prows.

Maple sugar making and a paper mill, typical New England industries, support the little town of Tyringham, nestling in a valley of the Berkshire Hills in western Massachusetts.

This simple white church amid the scrub pines of Cape Cod at West Barnstable, Massachusetts, is a good example of early colonial architecture. Here as elsewhere in traditional New England building, indifference to elaborate artistic concepts resulted in dignity and restraint.

Salem, Massachusetts, rich in the history and traditions of New England, is celebrated in stories of witchcraft and sea captains. Its Chestnut Street, laid out in 1796, today is considered one of the architecturally most beautiful streets in the country.

This is the interior of Christ Church at Cambridge, Massachusetts. Built in 1761, it was used in the Revolution as a barracks for American troops. A masterpiece of Georgian Colonial architecture, it is one of the most beautiful church interiors in the Boston area.

In the Munroe Tavern at Lexington, Massachusetts, are preserved the chair, table, dishes and hatrack used by George Washington during a visit there in 1789. The room is furnished just as it was when American officers were entertained there during the Revolutionary War.

87

Skiers gather on New Hampshire's White Mountain slopes during the long winter sports season, as indicated by this mid-April scene on the Boot Spur run in Tuckerman Ravine. Week-end "snow trains" bring excursion parties from New York and Boston to scores of such resorts.

88

Driving logs on the Swift Diamond River in northern New Hampshire is a dramatic phase of the state's lumber industry. More than three fourths of New Hampshire is woodland, and despite a sharp drop in lumber yield since 1910 timber remains its major natural resource.

Berlin, New Hampshire, on the Androscoggin River in the northern White Mountains region, is a lumbering and mill town in the heart of wild hunting country that offers bear, deer and game

Outstanding among the scenic spots of northern New England is Dixville Notch, two miles of alpine ruggedness and one of the showplaces of New Hampshire's White Mountain range.

birds. Near the Canadian border, the city has many residents of French origin. It is a skiing center and boasts the highest steel ski-jump tower in the world.

The Old Man of the Mountains at Franconia Notch, a formation of three rock ledges resembling a human face, is perhaps the most famed and most photographed New Hampshire scene.

Specimens of fine old colonial pewter-ware and furniture are housed in the early American room of the Currier Gallery of Art in Manchester, New Hampshire. From time to time during the summer the Gallery presents exhibitions of such items of interest as American blown, molded and pressed glass, early wrought-iron and wood utensils, colonial silver and Indian pottery.

The town of New Castle, New Hampshire, a few miles east of Portsmouth, retains the flavor of colonial days when patriots raided its fort to get gunpowder for Bunker Hill.

The rolling hills near Pownal Center, Vermont, are typical of the terrain in the southern part of the state where hikers start on the Long Trail through the Green Mountains. The Trail stretches 260 miles from the Massachusetts boundary to the Canadian border, with shelters, camps and

lodges along the way. The Green Mountains sprawl over an area that extends almost the entire length of Vermont. Their peaks are rounded, their forests heavy, and the green of their valleys is broken by streams and lakes.

95

Windsor, Vermont, whose rolling fields stretch westward from the Connecticut River, is the birthplace of Vermont. Here in the old Constitution House, then a tavern and now a museum, the state's constitution was adopted in 1777. Excluded for 14 years by the Continental Congress, Vermont in 1791 became the first state added to the original thirteen.

This large circular barn, with the traditional cupola on its roof top, is an example of a building style used in Vermont and elsewhere in New England early in the nineteenth century.

This sixteen-sided church at Richmond, Vermont, is a New England oddity, now is used only once during the year.

Old covered toll bridges date from the days when travel in Vermont involved payment to owners of rights-of-way.

From quarries near Rutland, Vermont, comes marble of quality unsurpassed in the Western Hemisphere. The state leads the nation in production of both marble and granite, which are in demand for monuments and public buildings throughout the United States.

Vermont's maple sugar industry has significance beyond its economic value — or even the lure of maple sweets. "Sugar time" is the New England equivalent of age-old spring rites. "Sap's a-runnin'" means an end to long winter and greeting to the never-ending cycle of the seasons.

Pawtucket, Rhode Island, an industrial town of some 80,000 population just above the northern tip of Narragansett Bay, typifies the many southern New England cities of similar size whose industries built up large fortunes in the nineteenth century. A metalworking center in colonial days, Pawtucket set the first American textile mills to turning after the Revolution.

The Marble Palace at Newport, Rhode Island, is one of the more spectacular of the imposing mansions that have made Newport known the world over as a showplace of wealth. Built of Vermont marble and stone from France, the house has a drawing room ablaze with crystal and gold, and its furnishings alone are valued at a million dollars. Newport was a social center as early as the Revolution, but it was in the years between the Civil and First World wars that it enjoyed its brightest splendor as a resort for America's wealthy.

This tree-sheltered roadway leading to a farm in Litchfield Hills expresses the charm of rural Connecticut. Dairy farms on wooded hillsides are a chief source of the state's farm income.

A farmer pitches a load of hay into his barn at Granby, Connecticut. The state's valleys and coastal plains are particularly suited to the growing of truck crops, potatoes and tobacco.

Beets, shown here in abundant growth on a farm in Torrington, are among Connecticut's important truck crops. Manufacturing towns in the state offer a ready market for produce.

103

A farm couple of Polish origin relish the livelihood they derive from tobacco. Along with its Yankee stock, Connecticut's population includes Irish, Italian, German, French and Slavic strains.

Over new beds on a tobacco farm in Connecticut, workers put up screens to protect the valuable plants. Connecticut shade-grown tobacco commands the highest price per acre of any crop grown in the United States. The state's tobacco today is chiefly wrapper leaf, but the first American cigars — known as "Long Nines" — were made in South Windsor in 1801.

Farm and Factory

THE STATES immediately below and to the west of the Great Lakes form a bloc of a half million square miles rich in natural resources and processing plants, compactly united by a network of rails, roads and waterways. These facts are familiar, but less widely realized is that the region has a singular beauty full of unexpected delights for the visitor prepared to shed preconceived notions.

The prairie is like the sea. Winds ruffle the tops of the grain, sending billows over its surface. Sun and shadow play upon the vast expanse with restless variety. Its flatness emphasizes the drama taking place in the sky, where clouds pile up and disperse, storms lower, break and recede. In the spring the prairie is black; in summer, yellow and green; in autumn, amber; and in winter, white with a whiteness that dazzles.

Many Americans, when they think of scenery, think of the coast of New England, the Florida Keys, the canyons of the Southwest, the heights of the Rockies or the groves of the Pacific Coast. But the Midwest, along with an elemental grandeur that accompanies great distances, has also the charm of flat rural country such as inspired the brush of many a Dutch, Flemish and English landscape painter. It has, too, the blue frame of the Great Lakes and the deep green of the northern peninsula.

On those who begin to understand the Midwest as well as see it, the area exerts another pull because it is one of the most typically American of regions. None can be chosen as typical of the United States as a whole if it has too rich a flavor of its own. This rules out crisp New England, the mellow South, the vivid Southwest, the opulent Pacific Coast, as well as the Rockies and the great ranges. In other words, it tends to rule out the outer or coastal sections and one intermediate section, leaving the heart of the country — the middle geographically, politically and socially — the Midwest.

107

At the center, the Midwest has acted as a fly-wheel to keep rival sections working harmoniously. After the Revolution, the acquisition of this great new territory compelled the fledgling states to strive toward a "more perfect union." Moreover, the settlers who crossed the Alleghenies to build up the commonwealth of Ohio and its sister states had passed through or come from New York and Pennsylvania, Central Northeast states whose role was to temper the rivalry of Massachusetts and Virginia. In the Midwest, energetic Yankee and easygoing Southerner met and fused. Abraham Lincoln, among others, was a product of this fusion. And although, with the question of extending slavery to new states, the dissension which led to the Civil War reached a crisis in the Midwest, the mere existence of the Mississippi basin tended to check any permanent cleavage between North and South.

Proof that the Midwesterner early became conscious of himself as an American rather than a colonist who had thrown off England's yoke, or an immigrant strongly bound to his homeland, can be found in the fact that he has preserved a native American pattern of living in folkways, manners, morals, customs, religion and politics. In character he tends to be straightforward, unpretentious, democratic, gregarious. He has vigor and enthusiasm which have served well his intellectual development.

With its prairies planted to wheat and corn, with what is left of great timberlands (once ruthlessly despoiled, now in places being reforested), with its wealth of iron and coal, great mills, packing plants and factories, the Midwest is also truly American in its economic pattern. Geographical location at the nation's core permitted the sensationally rapid development of its resources. It is usually a shorter haul by rail, road or waterway from the sources of raw materials in a given region to the processing plants of the Midwest than to those of other regions, and similarly it is a shorter haul from Midwestern plants to more great retail markets than from plants situated farther from the center. Thus the Midwest is the hub of the transcontinental railway system, and its regional capital, Chicago, is the railway center of the nation. The section's transportation is doubly favored by the prevalence of great waterways. Following after the frail canoes of the French explorers, vessels could come from the Atlantic via the St. Lawrence and the Great Lakes. And just beyond the Lakes were the great rivers descending to the Gulf of Mexico.

In 1850 Daniel Webster told the Senate: "Ere long the strength of America will be in the valley of the Mississippi." This vast expanse of prairie and timberland, a thousand miles wide

108

and more than a thousand miles deep, has been called the most richly endowed area of large dimensions in all the earth. That part of the valley which is the Midwest possesses a balanced plenty. Certainly when the nation was young it offered the greatest opportunities to industrious settlers: its rich black loam lured them on as later did California's gold dust. Like Russia's Ukraine, the Midwest is America's granary, the breadbasket of the country. But it is more; for today there are two Midwests, each equally important: the Midwest of fertile farms and the Midwest of productive factories.

Until development of the region's mineral wealth and the growth of processing plants caught up with and outshone its pre-eminence in agriculture, the Midwest could be thought of as a giant farm. In the years before World War II, Midwest fields grew three fifths of the nation's corn and one fifth of its wheat. The region's cows — the Midwest has twice as many purebred cattle as any other region — contributed half of the nation's butter, nearly three quarters of its processed cheese, two fifths of its milk. Half of all the hogs in the United States wallowed in its pens; and in its elongated chicken houses a third of the nation's chickens laid two fifths of the nation's eggs. The farmers of the Midwest fare better than other farmers: they have the most passenger cars, trucks, telephones and rural newspapers.

As if rich soil were not wealth enough, the region is heavily endowed with other natural resources. There are thirty thousand square miles of coal fields in Illinois alone. Bordering Lake Superior are iron and copper mines.

Today industry has outpaced the farm. Where farm workers formerly comprised 90 per cent of the population, they now make up only 40 per cent, the same proportion as for the United States as a whole. As a manufacturing center the Midwest is surpassed in quantity of production only by the Central Northeast, by far the most highly industrialized of all our regions. At that, the Midwest has a greater *number* of plants. Its cities, swinging in a wide arc from Cleveland to Milwaukee, have grown into world capitals for their particular products: meat in Chicago, automobiles in Detroit, flour in Minneapolis, rubber in Akron; elsewhere specialties range from beer and soap to cash registers and heavy machinery. The Midwest develops a third of the nation's horsepower. And in prewar years it had a quarter of the nation's wage earners, getting a higher average wage than that of any other region.

The center of population and industry in the United States during the Civil War period was in western Pennsylvania. But by the last decade of the century it had moved west to

109

Ohio, and today it has crossed the border of Illinois. The Midwest and its marginal belt accounts for nearly a third of the nation's retail trade, or only a little less than the Central Northeast and New England combined.

The region had its share of inventiveness. Minneapolis owes its pre-eminence to the discovery of a patent process of flour manufacture; a politician with a flair for mechanics invented the typewriter in Milwaukee; an Oberlin, Ohio, professor discovered the way to produce aluminum commercially. The first automobile in America was put together at Kokomo at about the time the first automobile was built in France. The first speedway was at Indianapolis. The Midwest produced Edison, Ford, Firestone and the Wright brothers.

It also produced vigorous writers: the greatest of all American humorists, Mark Twain; such sprightly columnists and versifiers as Eugene Field, George Ade, James Whitcomb Riley —men who embodied the dry wit and geniality of the true Hoosier; the murky but forceful Dreiser; Tarkington, popular delineator of youth; competent word-painters of the American scene like Willa Cather and Louis Bromfield, and the great contemporary folk poet, Carl Sandburg. Sandburg has succeeded in putting the essence of the region into words. Read, for example, these lines from *Cornhuskers:*

> Out of prairie-brown grass crossed with a streamer of wigwam smoke
> —out of smoke pillar, a blue promise—out of wild ducks woven in
> greens and purples—
> Here I saw a city rise and say to the peoples round world: Listen, I am
> strong, I know what I want.
> Out of log houses and stumps—canoes stripped from tree-sides—flat-
> boats coaxed with an ax from the timber claims—in the years when
> the red and white men met—the houses and streets rose.
> A thousand red men cried and went away to new places for corn and
> women: a million white men came and put up skyscrapers, threw out
> rails and wires, feelers to the salt sea: now the smokestacks bite the
> skyline with stub teeth.
> In an early year the call of a wild duck woven in greens and purples:
> now the riveter's chatter, the police patrol, the song-whistle of the
> steamboat.

110

If there is one city which more than any other epitomizes the development of a region where people who had grown up in log cabins spun out their lives in the shadow of the elevated and the skyscraper, that city is Chicago. It is the capital of the Midwest as much as New York is the capital of the Central Northeast, and the eight Midwestern states can properly be considered its hinterland. When, as early as 1673, the French explorer Joliet pointed out that boats could go from the Atlantic via the St. Lawrence and the Lakes to the Gulf of Mexico simply by cutting a canal through "half a league of prairie" at the portage of *Checagau*, he could hardly have envisaged the great freighters moving down the Chicago river to tap the wealth of the Mississippi Valley, nor could he have imagined present-day Chicago, a sprawling city of three million people, constituting the greatest concentration of population and wealth between the Atlantic and Pacific coasts and drawing to its terminals the railroads of a continent.

The skyscrapers of Chicago form an island, at the edge of the Illinois prairie, in which live and work forty-four out of every hundred residents of the state. Beneath the prairie is a vast bed of bituminous coal which makes the state even more important industrially than it is agriculturally. The value of its manufactures and raw materials qualified it for the place it already held by right of geography, the "First Province of the Middle Kingdom"—by virtue of enterprise, trade, its position as meeting place of North, South, East and West.

Historically the first province of the "Middle Kingdom," however, was Ohio, which at the time included what is now Illinois as well as what is now Indiana, Michigan, Wisconsin and the northeastern corner of Minnesota. Ohio is the natural transition from the Allegheny highlands to the great prairies. The two main routes to the West were the Ohio River, on the state's southern border—more serviceable than Boone's wilderness road through the Cumberland Gap—and Lake Erie, on the northern boundary. So valuable was the Ohio River artery that the English and French fought for its possession; and it was of tremendous importance in the development of the Northwest Territory. The second Pilgrim Fathers, a little group from Boston, founded Marietta on its banks; Revolutionary veterans built up Cincinnati; Cleveland was founded by Moses Cleaveland, leading shareholder of the Connecticut Land Co. which, like the Ohio Company, was formed to take over the lands of the Western Reserve. Half the population of the country can be found within a radius of seven hundred miles of Cleveland. Situated to take advantage of the iron ores from the Lake Superior regions, Pennsylvania's coal and the sandstone of the islands and southern shore of Lake Erie, situated also to serve as a

111

distribution point for finished products, Cleveland is a representative city of the Midwest.

Indiana also has coal beds overlaid with fertile soil. With the great steel centers of Gary, Hammond and Terre Haute it can hardly be called primarily agricultural, but its decentralized industrial pattern makes it a state of rural and small-town characteristics and its outstanding contribution to the American scene is quite possibly the Hoosier himself, good-natured, witty, a grass-roots American.

The state seal of Michigan bears the inscription: "If you seek a pleasant peninsula, look about you." Framed by the Great Lakes and essentially a part of them — four wash its shores — it is a land of undulating hills garnished with wildflowers, many trees except in the north where the cutover timberland is ravaged and desolate, copper and iron in the upper peninsula, and thousands of islands in its many streams and lakes. A land to attract the visitor from other regions, the state today takes its tone nevertheless from thriving Detroit, where workers build automobiles on the chain-belt system, from which salesmen go forth to spread the gospel of increased consumption and the ever-rising standard of living — which is one of America's substitutes for the challenge of the frontier.

Like Michigan, Wisconsin seems a part of the Lakes. Rimmed on the east and north by five hundred miles of Lake Michigan and Lake Superior, it is also bounded on the north by the rivers Menominee, Brule and Montreal, on the west by the St. Louis, St. Croix and Mississippi. Its southern boundary alone does not follow a natural watercourse. And within the state are more than four thousand lakes.

The climate, hot in summer but in winter as cold as northern Sweden or central Russia, made Wisconsin a natural habitat for settlers from northern Europe — Danes, Germans, Swedes. They brought with them an urge for liberty reflected in a progressive conception of statehood. They also brought their traditional skills which, along with grain fields and rich pastures for cows, helped Wisconsin lead the country in cheese factories, creameries and other dairy-products plants, thousands of which are run on the co-operative principle. Next to dairy products, malt and malt liquors have made the state and especially the thriving city of Milwaukee famous. The capital of Wisconsin, quiet Madison, was designed along the lines of the nation's capital, with radiating avenues. The campus of the state university, rising from Lake Mendota, is one of the loveliest in the country.

Minnesota was settled largely by hardy Swedes who still contribute many of its political

112

figures. The Twin Cities, Minneapolis and St. Paul, on the edge of the great Minnesota and Dakota prairie, became a wheat center, but today Minnesota farmers turn more and more to dairying. Agricultural co-operatives are more numerous here than in any other state. Social life revolves around rural organizations, and the event of the year is the annual picnic with its hog-calling, husband-calling, nail-driving and milking contests. Beauty is not lacking in Minnesota, especially in the thousands of maple- and birch-framed lakes lying amid the grain, below the big woods where grew up the legends of Paul Bunyan.

If it is no longer accurate to think of the Midwest as one great fertile farm, it is still reasonable to think thus of Iowa, which contains about 25 per cent of the first-grade farming land in the country and which consists of an almost monotonous succession of grain fields, sleek stock, well-kept barns and silos, and trim homes. It is a solid, prosperous land.

Mules, corn-cob pipes, showboats, flatboats, steamboats, "Show Me," Ozarks, Mark Twain, Daniel Boone, Jesse James, Dred Scott, Thomas Hart Benton—that is Missouri. A strange fate was reserved for the old French trading post of St. Louis, for a while held by the Spanish only to end up as what has been called "an island of Germanic culture in a sea of Anglo-Saxon indifference." Kansas City, Missouri, is a way station for the corn, hogs and oil of the nation.

These eight states, more alike in physical characteristics and more alike in what they represent than the states of any other region, make up the American Midwest. In its swift development, flowering meadows over which the Indians hunted were transformed into the most fertile grain fields in the world. A virgin territory as large as western Europe was broken to the plough, settled, united by steel and concrete. Its hidden resources were brought forth and transformed in huge plants that drew people together into great industrial cities. Today the prairie's yellow carpet stops short only of the mine tipple, the mill and the skyscraper.

113

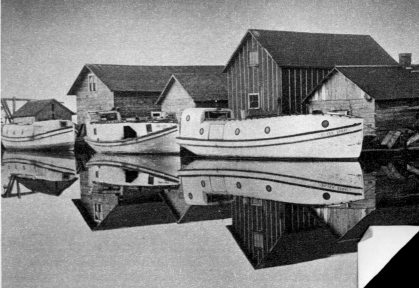

The Mississippi River, which forms the eastern boundary of Missouri, also shaped the state's commercial and cultural development, provided most of its romantic tradition. On it traveled the canoes of the French explorers, the flatboats of settlers carrying furs, salt, lead and iron to New Orleans, returning with necessities the frontier could not produce. The first steamboat went

downstream to Louisiana in 1811. In its wake followed tugboats, gaudy showboats and passenger craft that furnished the region's most luxurious means of travel. Recent years have seen a revival of traffic along the Mississippi, and excursion boats such as the *Queen of St. Paul* (above) traverse the waters made famous by Mark Twain's stories of river life.

Exploited by both the French and the Spanish, half slave and half free during the Civil War, Missouri has long been a land of conflict and controversy. Missourians even rose in dispute over the correctness of Thomas Benton's murals in the state capitol at Jefferson City.

Missouri led the region west of the Mississippi in education, opened the area's first school of college rank, first girls' school and first co-educational institution. The columns here, at Columbia, are all that remains of the state university's first building.

Iowa, typified by this Grundy County farm, has become a synonym for agriculture. A broad, flat state whose rural population exceeds its urban in all but 14 of its 99 counties, Iowa is blessed with wet springs, warm summers and a long growing season. Ninety-six per cent of its 56,000 square miles is in farms. The state leads all others in the production of corn, oats, hogs and

horses, in the number of corn-fed cattle and in the total value of grain crops, livestock and poultry. The State College at Ames, with science, engineering and forestry departments, grew out of agriculture. Its experiment station not only improves the quality of the state's produce but finds many new uses for the output of farms.

Iowa's position as a leading agricultural state has conditioned the life of its people. Existing by the land and their own physical stamina, they are sturdy, thrifty and tolerant.

It is a wealthy state, with a per capita income equaling the nation's average. The typical Iowa farm is modern both in equipment and in methods of cultivation. Money earned during boom periods is generally turned into building and land improvement or banked against leaner years. Among all the states of the nation, Iowa ranks first in literacy.

Originally a wheat state, Iowa switched to corn in earnest between 1893 and 1910. Since that time, through experimentation, yield tests and cross-fertilization, the crop has been developed until the state has raised more than 600 million bushels in a single year. Hybrid corn was first successfully produced in Iowa, in 1912, by Henry A. Wallace and Simon Casady of Des Moines.

Des Moines, Iowa's capital, has the air of a big small town. Its homes are fronted by broad yards and wide streets. Wooded areas can be seen from the downtown business section, open prairies from factory windows and from the old-fashioned, golden-domed capitol (above) overlooking the city and the Des Moines River.

Towering above the rim of Lake Bemidji in northwest Minnesota, Paul Bunyan and his famous blue ox, Babe, symbolize the prodigious strength of men who built the Midwest. Boasting lumbermen created this fabulous character to whom nothing was impossible. He pulled trees from the earth with his bare hands, scooped out Lake Superior for a reservoir to slake his thirst.

124

The footprints of his chore boy, lugging water from the reservoir to his master in the north country, formed Minnesota's thousands of lakes — whose fishing, canoeing and resort life today are one of the state's chief resources. Bemidji itself, once a lumbering town, now exemplifies the state's shift from timber products to manufacturing.

Like the trapper, lumberman and miner before him, the wheat farmer exploited Minnesota's natural resources to their fullest. Many farmers have since turned to dairying, but the state's rebuilt wheat lands still supply the world's largest flour mill at Minneapolis.

More spectacular even than Paul Bunyan is the Hull-Rust open-pit ore mine at Hibbing, Minnesota. Two and one half miles long, a mile wide and 350 feet deep at one point, it is the largest man-made hole on the face of the earth. Iron and dirt already taken from it exceed the 232,000,000 cubic yards of material excavated in building the Panama Canal.

126

Co-operative farming — as here on three farms operated as a unit — is widespread in Minnesota, often resulting in prosperity reflected by trim and well-kept buildings.

Herds of Guernsey cattle are as typical of Wisconsin's pastoral countryside as are her lakes and streams. Supplying the country with most of its Swiss cheese and a high percentage of all dairy products, the state's herds contribute greatly to the Midwest's abundance.

Wisconsin is one of the Midwest's great vacation lands. Its name signifying "Gathering Waters" in Indian language, the state contains 7,000 inland lakes, 10,000 miles of streams and rivers, is bordered by the Mississippi River, Lake Superior and Lake Michigan.

129

Chicago — the Windy City with its skyscrapers, Loop, stockyards, *Tribune*, North Shore and reputation for gang wars — sprawls between the Illinois prairie and Lake Michigan.

Chicago's heart is the Loop, seen on these two pages from the north and south sides of the Chicago River. The clock tower atop the Wrigley Building (opposite page) looks across the river to Wacker Drive and the Pure Oil Building at the left. Above, a tug steams up the river near the Wrigley Building, the Tribune Tower and the Continental Hotel.

131

As seen from the roof of the Drake Hotel, Chicago in midsummer takes on the appearance of a fashionable seaside resort. But Chicago possesses little swank. Oak Beach, backed by the high-living Gold Coast, is as friendly and unrestricted as are Jackson, Burnham, Grant and Lincoln parks, the Field Museum, the Art Institute and the Shedd Aquarium.

Chicago is too boisterous, too energetic, too busy to put on airs. The largest rail center in the world, the city has an industrial area containing more trackage than any one of thirty-nine of the nation's states. Thirteen miles west of Chicago in the Proviso Yard, the "hump" pictured above can break up, sort and dispatch a 100-car train in two hours.

Although Lincoln was born in Kentucky, spent his boyhood in Indiana and his most famous years in Washington, in the minds of the American people he is closely associated with Illinois. Saint-Gaudens' statue of the sixteenth President stands in Chicago's Grant Park.

134

Downstate in New Salem, where Lincoln lived, studied law and worked as a store clerk and postmaster, the thriving grist-mill village of 1830 has been restored. From the store whose replica is shown above Lincoln walked 12 miles to return an overcharge of three cents.

More than Lincoln memories have been restored with the tiny village of New Salem. From log houses like the one pictured here settlers went out to clear the new land and plant their crops, laying the foundation for southern Illinois' present agricultural prosperity.

Among Indiana's rolling hills and narrow valleys, her flat lands, lakes, sand dunes, back country and tiny hamlets, the most startling scenic note of all is the massive steel mills at Gary (above), Hammond and Terre Haute. Steel today leads the state's balanced industrial-agricultural economy which grew out of fur trading in the late eighteenth century.

The first permanent settlers in Indiana were the French Catholics at Vincennes whose descendants in 1825-26 built and dedicated the Romanesque St. Francis Xavier Cathedral.

137

TO COLUMBUS 17 ms.

To INDIANAPOLIS 43 ms.

TO FAIRFAX 25 MS.

To SPARKSFER 26 ms.

18.51   H. Cross

Since the wanderings of French Jesuits in search of Indian villages, Indiana has felt the great east-west travel of the nation. Today, all the major rail and highway routes between Chicago and the East pass through the Hoosier state. Above is an old signpost.

Herds of "whiteface" cattle, brought in from the West, grow fat across Indiana's lush central plain that stretches between the lake region in the north and the hills to the south.

Farming in Indiana is conducted on a smaller scale than in states like Iowa, Minnesota or Wisconsin. But fertility is high. Growths of oak, black walnut, beech, sycamore, yellow poplar, hickory, apple and cherry trees spread across the low hills and the central plain.

Probably no city in the Midwest better typifies the region's industrial importance and progress than does Detroit. Home of the automobile, Detroit first perfected the high-speed assembly-line principle of manufacture in plants such as River Rouge, whose power unit is shown above. Covering 1,200 acres, the Ford factory can build a complete car in less than 28 hours.

In a section of the River Rouge foundry, older students of the Henry Ford Trade School are given opportunity to make practical use of the theories learned in classrooms.

Detroit's sprawling Willow Run is evidence of the Midwest's manufacturing versatility. During war years, Liberator bombers rolled off the assembly line at the rate of one an hour. Today its facilities have been reconverted to the making of Kaiser-Frazer automobiles.

In contrast to industrial Detroit is the nearby Cranbrook Foundation's community. The Orpheus Fountain (above), by Carl Milles, is typical of the highly cultural nature of its five schools, church, stadium, observatory and outdoor theatre.

History has been preserved in Michigan by Henry Ford with reconstructed monuments at Greenfield Village in Dearborn. Above is a replica of the London jewelry shop of Sir John Bennett, watchmaker to royalty and government officials in the last century.

Thomas A. Edison's private steamboat, *Suwanee*, used on his vacations in Florida, is moored today at Greenfield Village, not far from a reproduction of Philadelphia's Independence Hall.

At the head of the Greenfield Village green stands the nondenominational Mary-Martha Church, whose bell was cast by Paul Revere. Here, too, Edison's laboratory has been rebuilt.

To supply industrial Detroit, freighters on the Detroit River bring a steady flow of materials —
ores, rolled steel, rubber, textiles, glass, paint, petroleum.

146

Rural Michigan bears little resemblance to its industrial cities. Scenes like this of a country church, an aged maple and farmers sowing seed are typical of its quiet farm lands.

Much of the early history of the Midwest attaches to its rivers, which contributed heavily in folklore and tragedy. Pictured above, at Cincinnati, is the Ice Gorge of the Ohio, down which traveled the city's founders. Quick to flood, plagued with fog, tricky currents and winter ice, the

river forms the southern boundaries of three Midwestern states — Ohio, Indiana and Illinois — before it spills into the Mississippi at Cairo. Once the main route for settlers moving westward, the Ohio is still an important shipping artery.

149

Ohio's urban population outnumbers its rural more than six to one. Yet along its low hills and rich river valleys spreads a panorama of rural well-being. Both the acreage and buildings of the state's hill farms are small . . .

. . . while the large-scale farms along the river valleys and in western parts of the state are larger and more diversified. Most of Ohio's produce — fruit, sugar beets, grapes, celery, onions, grain — finds a ready market in the state's many cities.

Rubber came to Ohio in 1910, turning Akron into a boom city and adding new products for the Buckeye State's vigorous economy. Ohio is highly industrialized, yet its steel mills, factories, coal and pottery towns possess a rugged stability.

Ohio's industrial growth began in the nineteenth century in small factories and mills lining the banks of her many rivers. It was not until the 1890's that heavy industry, concentrated in large cities along Lake Erie, supplanted such old mills as this at Foster.

Railroads and trucking companies have taken over much of the commerce that once belonged to the Ohio River. Pleasure cruises aboard old stern-wheelers are still popular, however.

Two of Ohio's inland waterways, the Scioto and Olentangy rivers, wind through the state capital, Columbus. Pictured above, beyond an arched bridge built after the 1913 flood, is the American Insurance Union Citadel, whose 47-story tower dominates the city's skyline.

Although the cities of Ohio are crowded with factories, the state possesses its share of architectural beauty. Rising before Cincinnati's Carew Tower, one of the highest buildings of the city, is the Tyler Davidson Fountain, pictured here.

154

The Plum Street Temple of Congregation Bene Yeshurun in Cincinnati is noted among American synagogues for its unique and colorful Moorish interior. Here, in the latter half of the nineteenth century, Rabbi Isaac Mayer Wise developed Reform Judaism in the New World.

Romance with Variations

JUDGING BY the quantity of documentation and description that exists on the subject, the people of the United States are more interested in the South than in any other region. Yet it is of all regions perhaps the least understood. Even many Southerners do not understand it. One reason lies in the hold the South has on the emotions of all Americans who know it or think they know it, tending to color interpretations which might otherwise be objective.

For some the South conjures up a stereotype of porticoes and pointed goatees, magnolias and mockingbirds, belles in crinolines, satiny thoroughbreds, faithful mammies and engaging pickaninnies, of places where the aroma of honeysuckle mingles with that of crushed mint. When the South is mentioned, some think of Virginia—the Old Dominion, mother of Presidents, birthplace of Jeffersonian principles and home of Jeffersonian architecture. To others it suggests the hazy outlines of the Blue Ridge; Negroes crooning in a shack by a cotton patch; the drone of the tobacco auctioneer; hill-billies using the language of the King James Version; stately avenues of live oaks wearing druidic beards; Mississippi river-boats tossing foam from their paddles as they disappear round the bend. It may mean street cries in languorous Charleston; pompano at Galatoire's in New Orleans' *Vieux Carré;* waterlily ranches; liners moving placidly through the sky along levee-born channels where the delta meets the sea. It may mean black water full of alligators, jungles full of orchids, egrets taking off for the next swamp, clippers taking off for Rio.

To others the South stands first of all for the Ku Klux Klan, Tobacco Road, Huey Long, hookworm, pellagra, child marriages, fundamentalism, boll weevil, cattle ticks, deserted lumber towns, coal and iron police, illiteracy, lack of leadership. Such a view is as much an oversimplification as the other. The traditional Southerners, in the words of Jonathan Daniels, are a "mythical people, created half out of dreams and half out of slander."

157

The fact remains that the South has a grip on our imaginations, and the reason may lie buried in our unconscious. It may be because the South is in many ways the most traditionally American of regions. In the land of cotton and tobacco, many descendants of early upper European stocks, undiluted by the successive waves of migration that affected other parts of the country, live a simple, rural existence characteristic of nineteenth century America. The "typical" Southerner is of British descent, lives in the country or in a small town, observes the Sabbath, takes his honor, his religion, his politics and his liquor seriously. He is remarkably consistent in his choice of creed and party. This isolated, almost patriarchal agrarian civilization has a strong if sometimes illogical appeal, especially to the harassed urbanite of other sections at grips with the complexities of a technological era.

Actually, the region defies simplification. It is complex and varied. In area and population it comprises about one fifth of the country; its eleven states cover the whole southeastern quadrant from the Atlantic to the Mississippi, as well as that area west of the river which is Arkansas and part of Louisiana. The Potomac and the Ohio are an approximate northern boundary and the Gulf of Mexico is the southern limit. Only about 30 per cent of the population live in urban areas, as contrasted with 75 per cent in the Central Northeast and New England, and the fourteen largest American cities are all in other parts of the country. The South has more cotton, more tobacco, more Negroes, more tenant farmers than all the rest of the country. It has the smallest farms and the largest families. And although the literacy rate is rising, it produces nearly as many illiterates as the remainder of the country.

The South is one of the country's richest regions in natural resources. Almost all of its more than half a million square miles is classified as suitable for crops, grazing or lumber. Rainfall maps show that all but a small fraction of the region lies in a belt receiving forty or fifty inches of annual precipitation — considered a "magic" one for the production of crops — and it boasts one third of the nation's area in which there is a growing season of six months without frost. The South possesses great wealth, much of it untapped, in water power, coal, iron and other minerals. It may be, as Dr. Howard Odum is fond of saying, that Southerners are often "the best people in the world doing the worst things." At any rate, all the South's potentialities can be developed readily by overcoming waste, deficiencies in skills, management and equipment (especially in farm buildings), as well as deficiencies in income, wages and industrial capital.

Even before the war years, the South had begun to show signs of swift industrial devel-

158

opment. Richmond claims to have grown faster industrially before World War II than any other American city, while Charlotte, Memphis, Atlanta, Norfolk, Miami and Jacksonville are among the seventeen fastest growing American cities in population, and the South shares with the Far West the distinction of being the most rapidly growing section in the country.

Dividing the South up into regions can become an absorbing game. The states, for example, tend to run in pairs, like foxhounds on a leash. Leaving out Virginia, since West Virginia, for the purpose of this book, is included in the Central Northeast, it is customary to couple North and South Carolina, which have the same equable climate and the same piny woods; Kentucky and Tennessee, with mountains, water power, horses and tobacco; Georgia and Florida's stretches of sandy coast, with their millionaires' playgrounds, and inland "cracker" country; Alabama and Mississippi, through which runs the great cotton-bearing Black Belt, named after black earth rather than black skin, although it might just as well have been the other way; Louisiana and Arkansas which have cotton, wood-manufacturing industries and the Mississippi River in common.

A rough division of the region into general areas might comprise the relatively flat tide-water section, for convenience considered as reaching all the way down the Atlantic coast; the highlands, with their Blue Ridge and Smokies; the Bluegrass region; the cotton belt; the Florida peninsula; the great valleys, Tennessee and Mississippi; the Gulf Coast, and, finally, the Delta. Each of these, of course, could be further subdivided into dozens more.

The states of Alabama, Mississippi, Georgia, Florida, Louisiana, and those parts of Arkansas and Tennessee bordering the Mississippi River constitute by self-definition a region-within-a-region known as the Deep South. David L. Cohn describes it as "poor, proud and prolific," an area which in the past "contented itself with producing large families, politicians, houn' dawgs, cotton, corn, sorghum, bee-martin gourds, hell-defying revivalists, and poetesses of the Confederacy." The Deep South also produces a bumper crop of writers who divide up about evenly into those who romanticize the past glories of an entrenched patriarchal — or perhaps more accurately matriarchal — social system, and those painting in somber hues the wretched estate of the cracker, the share-cropper, and the one-mule farmer. The Deep South is also the seat of the foremost Negro university. And the smokes and smells of the red ravines of the Alabama foothills are signs of its increasing industrial importance.

One fundamental difference that set apart the South from the North in early days was

159

that by and large the average planter and farmer was satisfied with the South and did not feel the urge to go farther afield than, say, Kentucky. If he had roamed an entire continent in large numbers like the restless Yankee, carrying his traditions with him, many of us would not have forgotten that the spot where the English first settled on this continent was Jamestown and not Plymouth. In other ways, however, the story of the development of the nation is as much the South's as New England's.

Managing a plantation called for competence and judiciousness of a high order, and it is no coincidence that the South gave us by birth or residence twelve presidents and fifty cabinet members before 1850 in addition to statesmen, orators and jurists of the calibre of a Patrick Henry, a Marshall or a Randolph. Few men bequeathed more to this nation than Thomas Jefferson, the Virginian, who wrote the Declaration of Independence and set up high standards in agriculture, science and education.

By 1850, however, the era of leadership was over. After that date, the South produced only two presidents, Andrew Johnson and Woodrow Wilson. And the course of events which its own leaders had chosen prior to that date — or had at least been unable to alter — was to involve the region in coils which still envelop it. For by 1850 the foundations had been firmly fixed for the South's plantation economy, farm-tenant system and biracial population. All are parts of one picture, of which the Civil War was the most dramatic highlight.

The story of the South is the story of cotton; and the story of cotton is the story of slavery. The war ended slavery but did not solve the region's biracial problem; nor did it solve the problems that beset a one-crop economy that had in part been a result of, and in part was responsible for, slavery. With all the wealth tied up in one crop, any bad guess might precipitate a crisis, and the planters made some bad guesses, as when they assumed Europe was totally dependent on them for its cotton supply. Other setbacks were to follow in their effort to keep King Cotton on his throne: leaching and erosion, exaggerated use of fertilizer, waste all around. The boll weevil made its debut. Other regions, especially Texas, began to grow cotton. There were three cotton "crashes" in the early part of the twentieth century.

The South's economic problems are on their way to slow solution. Its textile industry is now far larger than New England's; it has war-grown shipyards and aircraft plants, farming areas now devoted to apples, corn, peanuts, dairying, cattle and poultry raising. The trend is definitely toward a balanced economy that could conceivably set an example for the entire nation.

160

The South is also the home of our greatest experiment in publicly operated utilities, the Tennessee Valley Authority. Built at a cost of over three quarters of a billion dollars, this, the largest power-producing concern in America, puts back into the U. S. Treasury 13½ per cent annually on its investment while producing ten billion kilowatt hours of power. Ocean-going freighters now can ascend seven hundred miles up the Tennessee River. TVA dams have brought into existence nine thousand miles of new inland-water shorelines. Twenty thousand demonstration farms show the inhabitants of the valley how to use TVA phosphates; towns and farms in seven states benefit from its over-all program; power is already available in these states to increase production by three fifths. With these achievements go flood control of the waters of the Tennessee, erosion control and irrigation as well as recreational, housing and other civic improvements. It was President Roosevelt's dream to set up similar authorities in all the great watersheds of the country; TVA is showing the way.

The South's racial problem is still complex. Eight million Negroes, a third of the population, live in the South, and each race, white and Negro, is profoundly affected by the presence of the other. There are, in effect, two cultures existing side by side, each wary of the other, each bound, with respect to the other, by a complicated code of taboos and conventions.

Such organizations as the Commission on Interracial Co-operation have made a beginning toward resolving the distortions that such a system breeds. Perhaps new economic factors — greater wealth and better distribution of wealth, with resultant advantages in health and education — will be the strongest force in lifting a burden which old economic factors imposed.

Such questions, of transcendent importance to the South and all the nation, go deep beneath the surface. Even the casual visitor is aware of them, but only as an undertone, a shading of the South's surface flavor.

That surface flavor, to the dyed-in-the-wool Northerner, is felt strongly even in Washington, D. C., but the South really begins beyond the Potomac. One can feel its charm, very appropriately, by visiting Mt. Vernon, home of Washington, and by traveling thence through historic battlefields to Charlottesville, seat of one of the most superb groups of university buildings in the world, designed by Jefferson. Nearby is Monticello, the imposing Romanesque home he built in the foothills of the Blue Ridge; the little, unimposing home of Monroe; and Montpelier, home of James Madison, a mansion in true Southern style. Down the James, past beautiful old houses, lies Williamsburg. From Charleston, dozing beneath her oaks, it is a short

161

swing through a country of sand hills and tall pines to such resorts as Pinehurst and Aiken.

There is also the South of the highlands — the Blue Ridge sweeping from the Potomac to northern Georgia, the towering Great Smokies in North Carolina and Tennessee, the Alleghenies in Kentucky, the Shenandoahs in Virginia, the Cumberlands in Tennessee, the pine- and oak-clad Ozarks and Ouachitas beyond the Mississippi.

Your visit to the mountain regions may well start at Front Royal, Virginia, from which the Skyline Drive leads south through Shenandoah National Park. You can then follow the crest of the mountains along completed sections of the Blue Ridge Parkway to Asheville, resort center in western North Carolina. You may visit the haze-shrouded Great Smokies and drive almost to the peak of Clingman's Dome. The life of the mountaineers is worthy of investigation if only to ascertain that they are not all Jeeter Lesters.

To see the industrial South one should visit the great foundries of Birmingham which at night lie like a long black snake, winking red eyes. Georgia and Alabama will provide enough of the traditional old plantations, whereas many of those along the lower Mississippi have the piquancy of French style. The gulf ports are famous for their azaleas; New Orleans shares with Charleston and Santa Fe the distinction of having a flavor of the Old World.

If you can also manage to visit the tobacco country and the cotton country, you will have gained an impression of the South probably more realistic than you would from Hollywood productions or from the pages of overblown historical romances.

There are two sections in the South, however, which are not characteristic. They compensate by having as strong, if not stronger, atmosphere of their own. One is the peninsula of Florida, pointing toward the bright, Antilles-studded Caribbean and South America — and by no means lacking in the exotic color of those parts. The other is New Orleans and the Louisiana bayou country — the largest and most easily recognizable remnant of France within the confines of the United States.

There is the obvious Florida of winter sunshine, yellow beaches, warm water, palace hotels, skyscrapers, tourist cabins and gas stations, which has proved a magnet for hundreds of thousands, from millionaire sportsmen to retired civil service clerks. In St. Augustine, Ponce de Leon thought he had found the Fountain of Youth; today it seems to have moved to St. Petersburg, the trailer city, full of octogenarians quietly eking out their life span. Along the east coast are the earliest vestiges of Spanish colonization. There are old forts, sunken galleons,

162

and even buried treasure if you will look far enough. In the back country are the sleek, impassive Seminoles, sliding through dank everglades in dugouts to reach their wall-less houses on stilts. Farther down there is translucent indigo water off pine-covered keys haunted by deer; there are royal poincianas, Spanish olives and mangoes.

No less picturesque are New Orleans and the land of the Creole and Cajun in Louisiana —where even the ten-dollar bills had the French word for ten, *dix*, on one side—giving the South its colloquial name of Dixie. So perceptive a traveler as Count Keyserling found this region imbued with Gallic charm, and it has something even more than Gallic, with its iron-lace balconies, courtyards blooming with wisteria and camellias, its tradition of conviviality expressed in delicious cuisine and wines and in bacchanalian festivals that have become famous. In the old bayou country where cypresses grow in the water, and purple water hyacinths, live the Cajuns, simple peasant folk, descendants of the Acadians who were driven out of Canada, with their nostalgic folk songs and vigorous rustic dances.

In New Orleans and in Florida, however, you might well not meet as many examples of the typical Southerner as you would in, say, Kentucky. And in your ramblings about the South you will be lucky if you have come to know and understand him. He has a great deal to offer, but his make-up is not a simple one. He comes from a land where a good way of life has traditionally been considered more important than gain or even professional achievement, where dignity, form, good breeding and respect for the amenities were the rule. He is Democratic but not democratic; he habitually attaches some importance to family. Taking it for granted that all of us have enough leisure to enjoy life and be pleasant and courteous, he tends to be as disturbed by Yankee aggressiveness as the Northerner may be by what he takes to be Southern indolence. Both the proverbial hospitality and the class sense of the Southerner are epitomized in the remark made by the resident of a Georgia town when the question of putting up a hotel was under discussion. "We don't need a hotel," he said. "When a man comes here, if he's a gentleman, I'll entertain him. If he isn't, we don't want him in town."

163

The Kentucky Derby, oldest continuously held annual horse race in America and one of the nation's most colorful spectacles, has been run each year since 1875 at Churchill Downs in Louisville. The Derby is America's high point of pageantry in the horse-breeding and racing

world, in which Kentucky has long been a leader, and preparations for the race, as well as the result, are discussed with interest all over the country. At the track itself on Derby day, 25,000 spectators fill the stands and additional tens of thousands throng the infield.

A pair of hounds tree a raccoon in the hills of Kentucky, where hunting the animal with a pack of dogs is a major sport. Meat of the "coon" is a prized delicacy.

Thoroughbred horses, dear to all Kentuckians, have perhaps the nation's best breeding ground in the Kentucky Bluegrass region, where climate and soil elements foster strong bones and sinews.

167

The Natural Bridge near Lexington, Virginia, is a 90-foot span of stone over a 215-foot gorge cut by Cedar Creek. Thomas Jefferson acquired the site for 20 shillings in 1775 and built a two-room log cabin there for visitors whose names are still inscribed in a guest book.

168

The Luray Caverns in the Shenandoah Valley are the largest natural subterranean chambers in Virginia, contain remarkable stalagmites and stalactites. In a "room" called "The Cathedral," the formations resemble organ pipes.

In reconstructed Williamsburg, Virginia, dames in colonial gowns walk the Governor's Palace grounds. The House of Burgesses, at right, once housed Virginia's representative assembly.

Visitors to Williamsburg who look through the kitchen window of the Governor's Palace and call at the Raleigh Tavern (right) view scenes exactly as they were during the Revolutionary War.

The Governor's Palace was the residence of British royal governors from 1705 to 1775. After the Revolution, Patrick Henry and Thomas Jefferson occupied it as American governors of Virginia. In the decade following 1926, a nonprofit corporation financed by John D. Rockefeller, Jr., restored colonial Williamsburg according to Jefferson's plans.

The Devil's Head is a natural granite formation on Chimney Rock Mountain in the Blue Ridge range of North Carolina. Other features of the mountain, reached by trails and stairways from the base, are the Opera Box and Exclamation Point. Chimney Rock itself towers 225 feet.

172

The Great Smoky Mountains, part of the western Appalachian chain, are seen here from a point near Asheville, North Carolina. The Smokies, which adjoin the Piedmont plateau in the central part of the state, are tallest along the boundary between North Carolina and Tennessee.

Greenfield Lake, a former cypress swamp near Wilmington, North Carolina, has been developed into a recreational area with bathing and boating facilities. Surrounding the lake is a park where grow a wide variety of native flowers including the Venus's-flytrap, which "eats" insects.

173

Boone Hall, a plantation home near Charleston, South Carolina, stands on the site of an original homestead built in the late seventeenth century. Plantations with imposing main houses like this were the basis of the South's commercial rise before the Civil War, growing rice or cotton by slave labor for the industrial markets of the North and Europe.

The slave quarters at the Boone plantation have stood silent and empty since the emancipation of their inhabitants more than 80 years ago. Slaves were introduced into South Carolina from Barbados in 1671 after the colonists discovered the region's suitability for rice growing and the need for laborers who could resist the heat of the malaria-infested swamps.

The Middleton Place Gardens at Summerville, South Carolina, are probably the oldest landscaped gardens in America, surround the Butterfly Lake, shown above.

The Goose Creek plantation chapel near Charleston, South Carolina, is unusual in that it still bears the British royal arms. The Miles Brewton house (right) in Charleston was built in 1765.

This palmetto-shaped headstone stands in the yard of St. Helena's church at Beaufort, South Carolina. At right is the Pink House, a pre-Revolutionary tavern in Charleston.

176

Roadside scenes like this are common in the beautiful low country of South Carolina, where Aiken State Park, one of sixteen in the state, is located. In the region there are 1,700,000 acres of forest land. Aiken is also one of the nation's great polo-playing centers, the town and vicinity having a "population" of more than 2,000 polo ponies.

Watts Bar Dam, in Tennessee, one of several that maintain a nine-foot channel from Paducah, Kentucky, to Knoxville, is part of a vast system of navigational, hydroelectric-power and flood-control projects built and administered by the Tennessee Valley Authority. Begun in 1933 by the Federal government, TVA has virtually remade the Tennessee Valley.

This restored water mill, built in 1797, stands on a bank of Clear Creek in Tennessee, a striking contrast to the TVA's huge power project at Norris Dam, a short distance away.

The Parthenon, replica of the original Greek temple, stands in Centennial Park at Nashville, Tennessee. Constructed for the exposition of 1897, it was rebuilt in 1922.

Nashville, on the banks of the Cumberland River, is the capital of Tennessee and an important industrial center of the South. It is also the seat of eight major educational institutions.

Tennessee is divided by terrain and climate into three distinct regions. The upland east is much like New England, the central plateau like Ohio, and western Tennessee is "Deep South."

181

Surrounded by faithful hounds, an Arkansas hillsman fiddles a tune on the porch of his home in the Ozarks. Inhabitants of mountainous western Arkansas are regarded by sociologists as the purest Anglo-Saxon strain in the U. S. Their hill communities were untouched by nineteenth-century migrations and they still preserve songs and speech of Elizabethan times.

This view from Hot Springs Mountain shows a part of the city of Hot Springs, Arkansas, which contains a national park and where warm, medicinal waters flow from 47 springs.

The War Memorial Building at Little Rock, Arkansas, was the state capitol for three quarters of a century. It is considered one of the South's best examples of Greek Revival architecture.

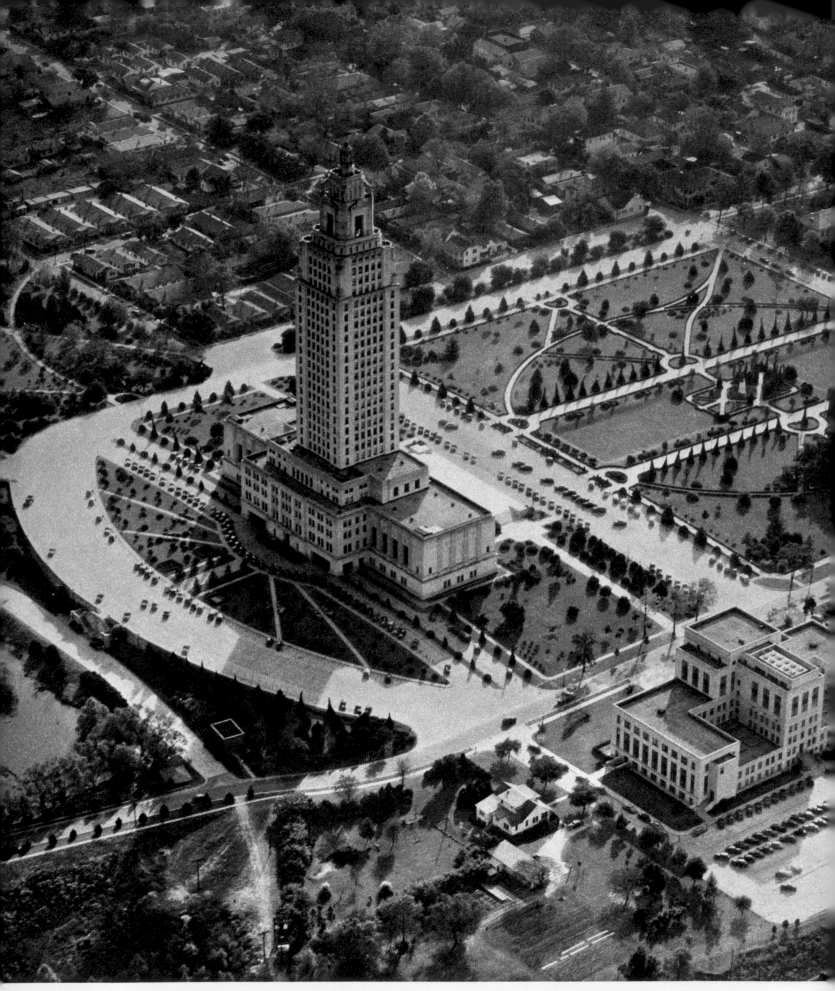

The skyscraper capitol of Louisiana dominates this air view of Baton Rouge, one of the nation's great oil ports. Refineries along the Mississippi River in the northern section of the city are among the world's largest, can handle 100,000 barrels of crude oil daily.

A moss picker of Louisiana's bayou country mans his flat-bottomed boat. Many inhabitants of the swampy lands adjoining the Mississippi river are "Cajuns," descendants of the Acadians who migrated from Canada and in many cases intermarried with Negroes or Indians.

Weird costumes and pageantry mark the annual observance of Mardi gras in New Orleans. This festival that springs from Louisiana's French tradition fills with hilarity the last hours before the penitential season of Lent. A parade of grotesque figures led by Rex, the Lord of Misrule, is the high point of the celebration which attracts thousands of revelers.

New Orleans, on delta land, interred its dead in surface tombs before modern drainage methods made burial underground possible. The custom still prevails.

French and Spanish influences appear in the walled patios (left) and wrought-iron balconies that characterize homes in the *Vieux Carré,* or French Quarter, of New Orleans.

Stanton Hall in Natchez, Mississippi, is one of the fine homes built in the South's era of plantation wealth. Completed in 1857 after five years' work, the house has a Corinthian portico, mahogany doors, carved marble mantels and huge inset mirrors from Europe.

Lumber at a sawmill on the outskirts of Natchez awaits shipment by Mississippi River boat. The lumber industry is the largest employer of labor in Mississippi, although cotton remains the most important product. More than half of the state's acreage is wooded.

About 1,500 pounds of cotton were needed to form this 500-pound bale of lint being trundled from a cotton gin in Alabama. After seeds are removed in the ginning process, the lint is compressed and baled for shipment. Alabama growers produce as many as a million bales yearly.
190

Blast furnaces cast their glow at Birmingham, Alabama, the major iron and steel producing center of the South. Development of the state's mineral resources during the last 30 years has created an important rival to agriculture as Alabama's chief enterprise.

191

Gardenias of the Cape jasmine variety are native to the entire South below Virginia. In Georgia, where they grow wild, many gardeners have developed the practice of banking them into massive hedges—showpieces of floral fragrance and beauty.

192

Georgia's coastal area, particularly the region between the Savannah and the St. Marys rivers, is noted for its magnificent specimens of live oak. Twisted and gnarled branches draped with gray Spanish moss cast intricate shadow patterns.

193

Sand, sea, sun and palm fronds form the setting for winter vacations in Florida which each year attract thousands of visitors from all over the U. S. and other parts of the world.

Cypress Gardens, bordering on Lake Eloise near Florida's west coast, are part of a recreational area developed in what was formerly a wild swamp. The gardens contain native and exotic plantings shaded by huge cypresses and oaks. Foot trails wind among the lagoons and flowers.

195

The Ringling Museum of Art is located in Sarasota, Florida, where the Ringling Brothers circus has its winter quarters. It is the state's largest art center and contains 700 original paintings by

European masters from classical periods to the modern. The museum building is constructed of Italian marble and incorporates architectural details from many historic European structures.

The reconstructed wooden balconies of the post office at St. Augustine, Florida, preserve the building's structural lines as depicted in a 1764 drawing. Beyond looms the tower of the Cathedral, completed in 1797 and restored after a fire in 1887. St. Augustine, oldest permanent white settlement in the United States, was established by the Spanish in 1565.

Alligators abound in the swamplands of Florida, are hunted chiefly for their hides. They will not harm a person unless molested, weigh as much as 1,200 pounds, live hundreds of years.

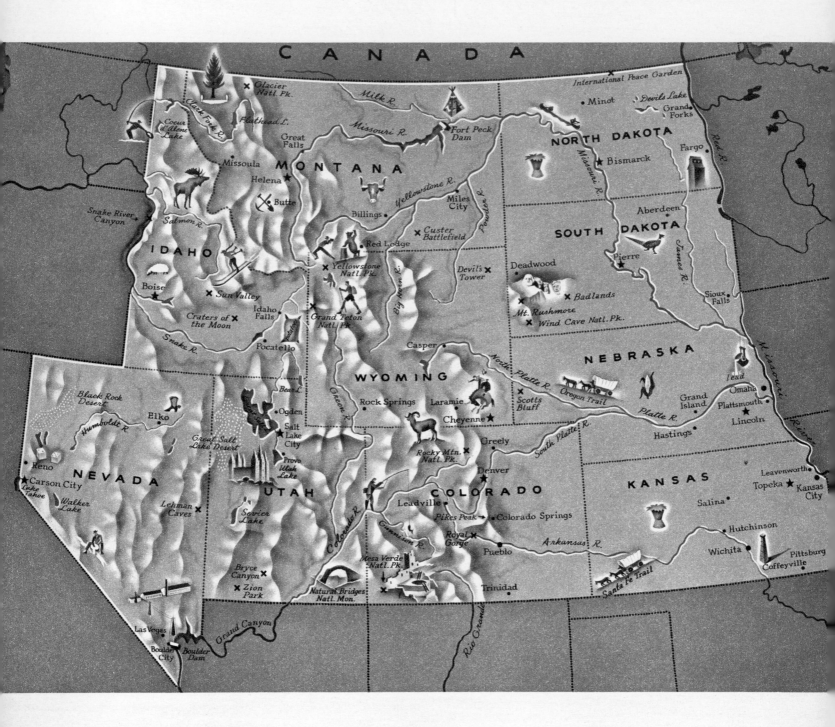

Mountains and Plains

WITH A THIRD of the total area of the country, the Central Northwest is the largest of the seven regions. Yet its ten states have only some 6 per cent of the country's population. The reason becomes clear when one considers the nature of the terrain. Arid plains and rugged mountain ranges were not inhabited until the tide of settlers on the coast began to flow back. The "Great Open Spaces" still justify the name.

Arm yourself with a pair of dividers and a map of the United States. Set the dividers at 500 miles on the scale. Place one point in Sioux City, where Iowa, South Dakota and Nebraska meet. With the other describe a circle. The northernmost point of the circle will fall a little short of Winnipeg, across the border in the Canadian province of Manitoba; the easternmost will take in Chicago; the southernmost, Oklahoma City; the westernmost will fall just short of Casper, Wyoming. Within this circle — a thousand miles in diameter — lies a relatively level expanse, fertile on the eastern side, arid on the west, which includes both the prairie country of the Mississippi Valley and the dry, dusty country of the Great Plains. The circle also includes the Ozarks, an edge of the Rockies and the Black Hills of South Dakota. However, this does not change the essential character of the area rising gently from the Mississippi to the Rocky Mountains. In Washington Irving's day the western half of the circle was a portion of the "Great American Desert," and General Zebulon Pike thought it would effectively prevent expansion to the west. As late as 1850 it remained a wilderness.

The upper states immediately west of the Mississippi — Minnesota, Iowa, and Missouri — belong to the Midwest, just as the states immediately to the west of the lower Mississippi — Arkansas and Louisiana — belong to the South. The Central Northwest begins with the states west of the Red River and the Missouri. Yet the eastern parts of North and South Dakota,

Nebraska and Kansas are essentially a continuation of the rich farm lands to the east. Toward the west the plain becomes drier, merging into the sand-hills region of western Nebraska, western Kansas and eastern Colorado; the jagged outcroppings of the Dakota badlands; the brown earth and sage-covered hills of Montana. Here the Midwest has given way to the West.

Roughly halfway between the Mississippi and the Pacific, the Great Plains blend into the foothills of the Rockies. Here the greatest mountain chain in the United States lifts its peaks from Canada to Mexico. Purple clouds gather around eagle-haunted summits; no less than fifteen hundred peaks are over ten thousand feet high. Here is the spiny backbone of the continent, carrying its great watershed, the Continental Divide. In Colorado and Utah the Rockies reach their greatest width — some three hundred miles — and their highest elevation — with fifty-one peaks in Colorado alone towering more than fourteen thousand feet.

Once they succeeded in crossing the Rockies, the pioneers must have wondered if they had not somehow blundered onto the steppes of Asia. The region between the Rockies and the Sierras is surely the weirdest in the United States. Horace Greeley, who urged young men to "go west," thought the area would be improved if these two ranges could be brought together and the intervening territory eliminated. Yet, while parts of it are dry and monotonous, others are strikingly beautiful. Idaho, for example, with desolate lava fields pitted with dead craters, interminable flats covered with sagebrush, also has rich, irrigated valleys, huge waterfalls, great forests. The picture-postcard quality of Utah is well known, with red and gray deserts, flat and peaked mountains, varicolored canyons. And if Nevada seems to consist mainly of alkali flats and gravel valleys, it also has ochre-tinted buttes, pine-covered ranges and glistening lakes.

A great inland sea, of which only the Great Salt Lake remains, once covered much of the region on the western side of the Rockies. The sea vanished, leaving a bowl so vast that the mountain chains within it fail to counteract the impression of hollowness. This is the Great Basin, the most arid section of the country. Unusual geological formations give it a moon-country appearance. At night the stars in the high, dry air glitter with intensity. The region has been called a land of "geology by day, astronomy by night."

Virtually up to the Civil War, buffalo roamed over the plains of the "Great American Desert," and at their heels the Indian warriors — Sioux, Blackfoot, Crow, Ute, Cheyenne and Kiowa — who relied on them for food, clothing and even fuel. The trails the buffalo made were utilized by the Indians on their ponies and later by immigrants in wagons. The first white men

202

to enter this country, however, were Spanish explorers pushing up from the south in search of legendary treasures. There followed French missionaries and trappers, then American traders sent out by John Jacob Astor and the Northwest Company. As early as 1804, Thomas Jefferson, who dreamed of America as a great agricultural empire, had sent Lewis and Clark to explore the region. Afterward came the covered wagons moving slowly along the great trails — the Oregon, the California, the Mormon.

Few chapters in the epic of America's unfolding are more dramatic than that which describes how the Mormons envisioned a re-creation of ancient Palestine, the Red Sea, the Jordan, in the deserts and valleys of Utah. "This is the place," their prophet said of a parched tableland where no one else had settled or believed it possible to exist. The Mormons brought water, planted and ploughed with sober persistence, divided the land into small farms and helped each other unselfishly. Today shade trees, green fields and trim cottages in Utah indicate a Mormon settlement. These pious laborers prospered and eventually acquired other riches than the yield of the soil, making them the rulers of Utah and an influence in the life of the nation.

One thing the soil of the Great Plains would support from the beginning, without Mormon coaxing or machine-age equipment, was cattle. From the great southwestern ranges enormous herds urged on by cowboys had been making their way hundreds of miles north to railheads in Kansas. Then, one winter during the Civil War, a teamster caught in a snowstorm on the plains of Wyoming turned his oxen loose, only to find them again in the spring sleeker than ever. From that time on, thousands of steers were fattened on the nourishing northwestern grasslands, and Colorado, Montana and Wyoming — which soon came to rival Texas in the tradition and atmosphere of the cow country — were brought within the confines of the cattle empire.

Little is left today to mark the route of the old trails — the Chisholm, the Pecos, the Goodnight, the Bozeman — except where stunted stands of corn show where the soil was packed hard by a thousand hoofs. The old railhead cowtowns have lost some of their flavor. But in the Central Northwest, cowhands still ride the range much as they did in the old days, round up cattle and, if they seldom "shoot up the town," still relax with guitar and drawling songs.

Gradually even the plains began to attract dissatisfied, restless or ambitious farmers from the Pacific Coast and from the Midwest, just as every successive frontier had in its day. Some made a bare living, but many had to abandon their sod houses after a fruitless struggle. Success in farming this dry country had to wait for technological development — for tools, wire, wind-

203

mills and railways. With these facilities, it became possible not only to exist on the land but to gain wealth from it, and there came the period of great farms extending over thousands of acres, often ruthlessly exploited by investors who did not themselves take part in the struggle. This exploitation, like that of the forests and the mines, led to tragic results, for a large part of the region became the "Dust Bowl," where nothing would grow and from which impoverished farmers and share-croppers had to flee after years on the land. But in modern days the storing up of water by means of dams has brought renewed fertility to a thirsty region. Uncompahgre Dam has reclaimed 63,000 acres in southwestern Colorado. Arrowrock, in Idaho, is one of the highest dams in the world. The problem of farming the plains, learned at the cost of so many frustrated hopes, is on the way to being solved.

The soil was looted, yes. But not the soil alone. In this rugged country were immense riches beneath the earth's surface, veins such as the Comstock Lode, from which twenty-one million dollars worth of silver was taken in the first year of operation, 1873. Since the eighties, a fifth of all the copper mined in the United States has come from a few square miles around Butte, Montana. The city's businessmen today, looking out from skyscraper offices in a strange mixture of shafts, dumps, clubs and churches, pride themselves on living in "the biggest mining camp in the world." Recently Utah has begun to catch up with Montana and Colorado as one of the leading mining states, with Salt Lake City one of the great smelter centers of the world.

There is one other richness with which the Central Northwest is lavishly endowed — natural beauty. In this thinly settled region, containing much of the most striking mountain scenery in America, it has been possible to set aside vast areas as national parks. In the northwest corner of Wyoming lies Yellowstone, first national park anywhere in the world, largest and best known in America, a wilderness of thirty-four hundred square miles. More geysers are to be found here, it is claimed, than in all the rest of the world; a waterfall — among many — twice as high as Niagara; canyons as colorful as the Grand Canyon in Arizona; petrified forests; icy lakes and lakes of boiling mud; woods, valleys, rivers and mountains of great beauty. The majesty of the Alps is equaled in western Montana's Glacier National Park, where rocky shelves of mountain masses are studded with sixty gleaming glaciers.

In Colorado's Rocky Mountain National Park you can climb to the "roof of the world," learn the true character of the Rockies in the bleak grandeur of their bare, wind-swept summits and snow-sheathed gorges. In South Dakota, a puny youth named Theodore Roosevelt hunted

204

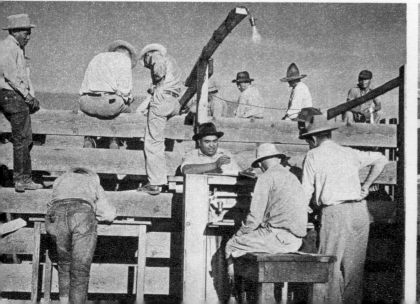

his way back to health among the tinted ravines of what the French explorers contemptuously referred to as the *Terres Mauvaises* — the Bad Lands — now a national monument. Utah offers the colored walls of Zion National Park and the temples of Bryce Canyon, whose pillars of old rose are kindled into flame by the sun.

For the vacationist the Central Northwest provides resorts to every taste. Those who relish comforts amid grandiose scenery will appreciate Colorado Springs. The mountains are cloaked in color, and the hard bright sun shines down through tingling air. For those who like to skid down a ski slope in shorts, plunge into a glass-enclosed pool, or listen to the latest "name" band, there is Idaho's Sun Valley, a year-round center for recreational sports. In contrast there is good sailing on Lake Mead in Nevada, back of Boulder Dam.

Everyone knows that Nevada is the state where divorces can be obtained with speed. It is also a land of gaming tables and conviviality, of bars in every café. Climatically, however, it is the driest state in the Union. Of its area, 95 per cent is unproductive except as grazing country for cattle and sheep, and only 1 per cent is irrigated. Although it is more than twice the size of either New York or Pennsylvania, Nevada is really one enormous stock ranch, its open spaces relieved at infrequent intervals by gay, frontier-type towns.

The Central Northwest was literally the nation's last frontier. With the exception of Colorado, admitted in 1876, none of the states was admitted before 1889. At last the frontier ceased to play a determining role in the growth of the country. But it remained an important factor in the American point of view. Out where the plains stretch to the circle of the horizon, where between chains of pinnacled mountains are valleys so vast you could "drop Delaware or Rhode Island into them and never miss them" — in the land where the pattern was set by the miner, the cowhand, the sheepherder, the copper baron, the cattle king, the seeker of adventure — the frontier habit of thinking endures. And, because many traces of the frontier outlook also persist among Americans in all parts of the country, the "Great Open Spaces" are significant as a symbol. They are part of our national myth.

Boulder Dam, which backs up the waters of the Colorado River into Lake Mead in the southern corner of Nevada, is the highest dam (726 feet) ever built by man — the core of a vast power and irrigation project serving Nevada, Arizona and California. Begun in 1928 and put into operation in 1936, Boulder has an ultimate power-generating capacity of 1,322,300 kilowatts.

Lake Mead, stretching 115 miles upstream from Boulder Dam, is the largest artificial lake in the world. Its recreational facilities rival Boulder's irrigation and power operations in scope. Sailboats the year around skim over the lake's surface and into the several canyons the waters have partially filled. The chief sports and camping center is at Hemenway Wash.

Virginia City, where fortunes were made and lost overnight in gold and silver rushes, is perhaps the best known and most storied of Nevada's landmarks.

208

This statue on the facade of the courthouse at Virginia City is unique in that it shows Justice with open eyes and balanced scales. Virginia City was the scene between 1860 and 1870 of silver and gold discoveries that had far-reaching effects on the nation's economy. Wealth derived from them helped pay the Civil War debt and finance the Atlantic cable.

Cathedral Gorge, a chasm of remarkable coloring in southeastern Nevada, is so named because the formations carved by wind and rain in its soft, chalky clay resemble architectural spires.

The shifting sands of Death Valley, which overruns Nevada's southwestern border into California, have long been famed as a wasteland that has trapped many a traveler. Sinking to 279.8 feet below sea level, the valley is the lowest point in the United States, but from its floor can be seen 14,495-foot Mt. Whitney, highest point in the U.S.

211

Sun Valley, a year-round vacation resort 6,000 feet up in the Sawtooth Mountains of Idaho, provides a wide variety of sports. Winter and spring furnish powdery snow on treeless slopes for skiing, ski-joring, tobogganing and dog-sledding.

Outdoor swimming in warm-water pools is possible even in midwinter at Sun Valley, when other activities include skating and riding in reindeer-drawn sleighs. During the summer, game fishing, golf, tennis, horseback riding and pack trips are popular.

212

Coeur d'Alene Lake lies in the heart of a recreational area of exceptional beauty in northern Idaho. Its shores are the summertime scenes of boating, swimming and water-skiing, and facilities for camping and fishing are abundant on its wooded shores.

Symbolizing Utah's major industry are the superstructures and workings of the open pit copper mine in Carr Fort Canyon. The mining installations extend for several miles up the gorge.

214

A broom maker bearing an armful of broomcorn personifies one of Utah's minor industries, an offshoot of the state's agriculture. The principal crop is sugar beets, with wheat, oats, barley, potatoes, hay, alfalfa and rye all furnishing important yields. Fruit and vegetables also are grown in profusion, and Utah grasslands nourish some 2,200,000 sheep.

Mesas and buttes varying in height from 800 to 1,200 feet, jutting at intervals from the desert floor, present strange and enchanting panoramas in the Monument Valley of southern Utah.

This view, from Comanche Trail, of the strange formations of Bryce Canyon, with Sunrise Point in the distance, indicates the topographical splendor of Utah's Bryce Canyon National Park.

216

These huge twin arches in the Windows section of the Arches National Monument in Utah are one of the most unusual features of the Central Northwest. Carved by wind and sand through the ages, these natural bridges are so large that a fifteen-story building could fit easily under the nearer arch. Note the man silhouetted against the sky under the farther arch.

217

The Utah Copper Company's mine at Bingham Canyon constitutes the largest open-pit copper diggings in the country. During the war period, one third of the nation's total domestic copper production originated here. Utah ranks first among the states in total ore output and in gold production. It holds second place for copper and silver.

218

The interior of the state capitol building at Salt Lake City, Utah, contains murals depicting the state's development since the Mormons established their religious community here in 1847.

This view of the mountains in the Pikes Peak region indicates the nature of Colorado terrain.

Unaweep Canyon, its Indian name meaning "canyon without a head," lies in southwest Colorado, stretching away from the Uncompahgre Plateau in a country of magnificent distances.

Pikes Peak, the snow-covered height shown above, is famed in Indian legend and pioneer lore.

Snowmass Peak, overlooking Snowmass Lake in Holy Cross National Forest, is one of Colorado's most graceful heights. Colorado's mean altitude of 6,800 feet exceeds that of any other state.

Two hunters advance cautiously on their prey after felling a 700-pound elk near Gunnison, in one of Colorado's best recreational areas. Trout-fishing is also excellent in this region.

This black bear, photographed in the Rocky Mountain National Park, is one of a species still fairly numerous in Colorado although not often so readily observed. Rocky Mountain bighorn sheep, mule deer and elk can also be found in the 250,000-acre park. Grizzly bear, mountain lion, coyote and bobcat are seen infrequently.

Framed through an arch of the Colorado state capitol, Denver's civic center extends toward the city and county building in the background. Denver is known as "Queen City of the Plains."

A worker tends the flotation process at the Golden Cycle Mill in West Colorado Springs, the largest plant of its kind in the United States for the treatment of gold ore. More than five million dollars in bullion has been shipped from here in a single year to the mint at Denver.

The falls of the Yellowstone River are one of the many spectacular sights which annually attract hundreds of thousands of visitors to Yellowstone National Park in Wyoming's northwest corner.

The Chapel of the Transfiguration near Jackson, Wyoming, is an example of the rustic building style predominant in the Jackson Hole country, where frontier atmosphere is fostered for the benefit of visitors. In the background rise peaks of the Grand Teton Mountains.

227

These sheep, drinking at a watering place on the Wyoming range, comprise a few of the more than 3,500,000 head that graze on the state's prairies, ranches, farms and national forests. The first sheep were brought to Wyoming in 1845, and in the last 100 years the herders waged a long struggle against the natural hazards of their lonely work and against rival cattlemen.

228

Today, Wyoming ranks second only to Texas in the production of wool and mutton, and selected Wyoming sheep are shipped all over the world for breeding. With scientific handling methods, community shearing and dipping pens and modern appliances for his wagon home, much has been done to improve the sheepherder's lot, but little can change the loneliness of his life.

The Devil's Tower, a cylindrical rock mass rising above the Belle Fourche River in the Black Hills region of Wyoming, is one of the state's most conspicuous geological features and the first U. S. national monument. Rising 600 feet to a nearly flat crest varying from 60 to 100 feet in diameter, the Tower is a lava formation some 20,000,000 years old.

Horse raising is a major industry in Wyoming, where mounts are needed for the cattlemen who produce a large share of the state's wealth. The cattle themselves are bred for efficiency in turning feed into beef, and also for yielding a maximum of the higher priced cuts.

Draw poker, with wooden matches for chips, is the standard amusement of cowboys in their leisure hours. Here a group enjoys a hand in the bunkhouse of their ranch near Casper, Wyoming, where a celebration is held annually reviving the spirit of the state's frontier days.

231

White trumpeter swans, a species almost extinct in the United States, nest in the 50,000-acre bird refuge at Red Rock Lakes, Montana. Pelican, too, are sometimes seen and great blue herons are common in summer. Among other species are canaries, meadowlarks, bobolinks.

Going-to-the-Sun Mountain, so named by the Blackfeet Indians to whom the Great Spirit sent a legendary leader and called him back to the sun from this spot, is the climactic point on Going-to-the-Sun Highway, one of the features of Glacier National Park in western Montana.

Built by gold prospectors in the early 1870's and abandoned little more than a decade later when pannings petered out, Cooke, Montana, was an isolated ghost town for 50 years until highway construction brought its now-historic buildings within reach of travelers.

This log courthouse at Cooke was built during the town's brief heyday as a gold prospecting center. The first miners, with the crude methods of their times, missed much of the valuable ore found in the area. Gold dust can still be panned on a moderate scale.

234

A grandmother of the Blackfeet Indian tribe smokes a pipe outside her tepee on a reservation covering 2,343 square miles in northwestern Montana. The Blackfeet, governed by an elected council of 13 members, were among the first Indians to adopt a constitution for self-government.

On the Skyline Drive in Dinosaur Park loom life-size replicas of the prehistoric monsters that roamed what is now the Black Hills region of South Dakota. The Black Hills, apparently formed by a geological upheaval distinct from that which resulted in the Rocky Mountains, today are a rich recreational region, abounding in fish and wildlife.

The Bad Lands of South Dakota cover a million acres of some of the most unusual geological formations in the world. Layers of sedimentary deposits from the floor of a prehistoric salt sea are piled in almost every conceivable pattern of line and color to heights of more than 500 feet. Two roads afford generous views of fantastic peaks and gullies.

The heroic features of Washington, Jefferson, Theodore Roosevelt and Lincoln, carved on a mountainside in South Dakota's Black Hills, constitute one of the world's most familiar monuments — the Mount Rushmore National Memorial. The work of the sculptor Gutzon Borglum,

the heads are some 60 feet in height, proportionate to men 465 feet tall, and stand at an elevation of 6,200 feet. Because of its patriotic conception, the memorial has come to be known as the Shrine of Democracy and is viewed by more than a million visitors each year.

Farm lands stretching for miles over the plains near Fargo, North Dakota, suggest the nature of the vast American grain belt of which this state provides the northernmost link. North Dakota's chief crops are wheat, corn, cane, oats, rye, barley, flax and the hardier fruits, with the production of livestock also a feature of the state's agriculture.

The North Dakota state capitol at Bismarck, one of three of skyscraper height in the country, is the arena for the progressive politics with which Dakota farmers tackle the agricultural and economic problems of their region. In addition to its political importance, Bismarck is a major shipping point and trading center for the surrounding farm area.

Turkeys thrive on the dry, sunny climate and extremely fertile soil of Nebraska, which lends itself to the raising of a wide variety of stock. The state has more than 2,000,000 swine.

Havens, which proclaims boldly its population, is one of hundreds of tiny communities that dot Nebraska's plains and are supported by grain fields, farms and cattle ranges.

The stockyards at Omaha, which surround the Stock Exchange Building of the Nebraska metropolis, are the nation's third largest livestock handling center. Omaha has supplemented its rapid industrial growth with an impressive civic improvement program.

A cowboy hits the dirt after a short-lived attempt at bareback-riding a bucking steer during a rodeo at Valentine, Nebraska. Though Nebraska today is given over largely to the cultivation of grain, its past is rich in the history of the West's cattle industry. Cattle are still an important factor in the state's economy, with meat packing one of the most important industries, and the cattlemen's traditions are kept alive by displays of riding and roping skill such as are held from time to time throughout the West.

Grain storage towers adjoining railroad tracks are the points of departure for the Kansas harvest to U. S. and world markets. The state annually produces 170 million bushels of wheat.

Prize Hereford bulls like this help Kansas maintain its rank as one of the nation's four top cattle raising states. Kansas has nearly three million cattle, including 500,000 dairy animals. The state is famed in cattle history from the days of the Chisholm Trail, over which herds were driven from ranges to railheads in operations comparable to a military campaign.

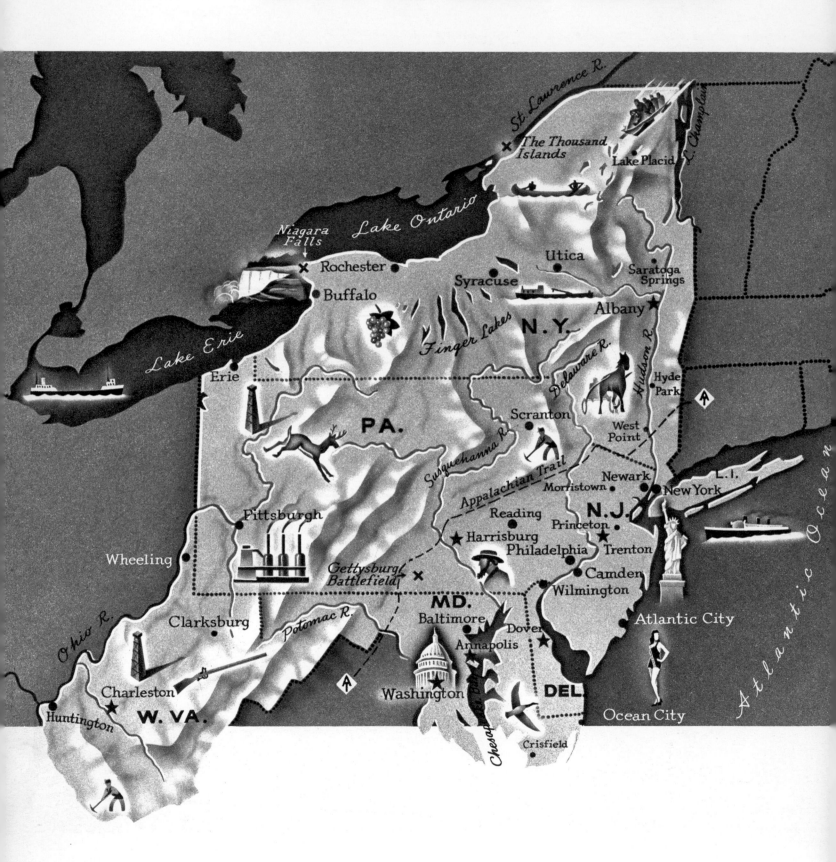

Wealth and Industry

Fifth Avenue and Forty-second Street in New York City comes as near as any single point to being the exact center of this planet's surface. Skeptics might ask: Is there any valid reason why a population greater than that of Sweden, Peru, Greece or Australia should live and work packed together on 200,000 acres, an area so small that the only direction expansion can take is up into the sky?

There is. The only possible explanation is the correct one. People crowd into New York City because today it is the capital of the world. It is the capital of wealth, ownership, philanthropy, industry, commerce and trade. It may also become the political capital of the world. Moreover, it is the nerve center, the world capital, for better or worse, of ideas, culture, fashion, education and art, and the essential business of disseminating these intangibles.

In describing the metropolis, superlatives lose their impact. New Yorkers do not need to boast and point with pride. They can pay their city the supreme tribute of ignoring its immensity and treating it with the casualness appropriate to the small town.

New York's pre-eminence is shared by its hinterland, which comprises two layers, the upper layer being the states of New York, New Jersey and Pennsylvania, the lower composed of Maryland, Delaware and West Virginia. For statistical purposes, New England is often included, making still another layer. In the years before the Second World War, the Central Northeast and New England, with 6.9 per cent of the nation's land area and a little under a third of its population, had nearly 40 per cent of the national income. But in finance and industry their proportion was much greater than that of any of the five other regions. The Central Northeast and New England received more than half of the total U. S. income from finance; from manufacturing, roughly 45 per cent; from building, government, utilities, trade

249

and service, 40 per cent; from mining and quarrying, just under 40 per cent; from other sources, over 43 per cent. Even in agriculture their share of the total income was exceeded by only two other U. S. regions, the Southeast and the Midwest.

If you took a map of the world and on each country placed a pile of quarters, each quarter standing for a billion dollars of estimated wealth, the tallest pile would be the one placed squarely on the United States. If you repeated the process with a map of the U. S., placing a pile of quarters on each state, the tallest pile would be the one on New York State. And of course if you broke down New York State by counties, the county of New York would get the tallest one. It would now make sense to shove this pile down to the tip of Manhattan Island until it came to rest in Wall Street between the old Treasury Building and J. P. Morgan and Co.

New York banks clear more than half of all U. S. checks. The nearly 8,000 commercial vessels visiting the harbor each year carry over 40 per cent of all U. S. foreign trade and more than half of all U. S. imports.

In the less tangible realm of ideas, policies, modes and manners, culture and art, the predominance of the Central Northeast and its metropolis can hardly be demonstrated by statistics. But of the three great media for the dissemination of ideas, at least two center in New York: the press and the radio. The creative expression of an entire country is funneled through the city which, aided by Boston and Philadelphia, publishes most of the country's books and magazines and alone produces its plays, markets its pictures, sets its musical and radio standards. In the main, New York also tells the nation's women what they must wear.

The essence of New York is sophistication. The essence of sophistication is not to be surprised at anything. At one end of the scale of moral qualities this may be called being blasé, at the other end, tolerance. You are not surprised at another's ideas or way of life, nor shocked by them; you allow him to work them out. Tolerance was a characteristic of the Central Northeast — as distinguished from New England and the South — from the earliest days.

The origins of the Central Northeast were cosmopolitan rather than purely English. New York had its Dutch and Huguenots; Pennsylvania its Germans from the Palatinate, Swedes, Welsh and Scotch-Irish. During the nineteenth century, when Europe began sending a horde of immigrants, New York, gateway to America, and its hinterland kept this cosmopolitan character. Nearly five million of the country's eleven million foreign born live in the Central Northeast. Immigrants and the sons and daughters of immigrants make up five

250

eighths of the population of New York City. It is the greatest Jewish city in the world, the largest Negro city. New York has more Irish than Dublin, nearly as many Italians as Rome, and many other and more exotic nationalities huddled together for the most part in tenement areas. Industrial Pennsylvania, too, has filled up with factory workers from all parts of Europe. The resultant mixture of races and nationalities relieves the Central Northeast of any suspicion of provincialism.

In addition to being a magnet for Europe's working classes, New York City is a lodestar for Americans. For a place where the hand of man has obliterated practically every vestige of natural scenery, it is the greatest host in the world. Leaving commuters out of the picture, it shelters as many visitors each day as the entire population of Knoxville, Tennessee, or Wilmington, Delaware — generously over a hundred thousand. In a year the number totals over four million, who leave behind nearly two hundred million dollars in hostelries and in varied and presumably stimulating places of entertainment. In place of natural scenery the metropolis has a man-made skyline which is breath-takingly dramatic, whether seen in the almost Mediterranean sunshine of an autumn afternoon or by night when it brightens the sky with millions of electric lights.

Although at first glance the predominance of New York would seem to be based primarily on financial control, an equally good case can be made to prove that it is based on the production of iron and steel. Pennsylvanians choose that side of the argument, and they can make a good case to prove that the most important state in the Union is not New York but Pennsylvania.

The smoke of Pittsburgh's blast furnaces represents the might of the U. S. even more than do the green baize tables of Wall Street. In the history of the country, that smoke stands for iron, steel, coal; the development of the crafts; manufacturing and the privileges of skilled labor, and for the swift climb in industrial production. For at least half a century Pittsburgh has produced half the country's output of steel rails, coke, plate glass, glassware, iron pipe. Her tonnage by river and rail is greater than that of any other city in the world. The city is the home of the world's greatest Bessemer steel plant, crucible steel plant, rail, tube and freight-car works, producing armor, shells and instruments for the world's navies, bridges for the Far East, locomotives for South America. Fifteen per cent of the bituminous coal mined in the U. S. comes from the Pittsburgh area, and all of the country's anthracite is mined in one 484-square-mile

251

patch in east-central Pennsylvania. The Keystone state alone accounts for 10 per cent of the total value added to products by manufacture every year.

In addition to her mineral wealth, Pennsylvania has the richest agricultural land of its extent in the world: the loams of rolling Lancaster, York, Berks, Bucks and Chester counties.

These fertile regions also are the home of many of the remaining racial groups in this country which preserve their traditions, their costumes and their folk art. Here you will find the sober "Pennsylvania Dutch," with his great barns protected by "hex" marks, his furniture painted with gaudy Zoroastrian tulips; the Mennonites in their shovel hats; the "beardy" Amish, who use hooks and eyes on their costumes of brown homespun because buttons are considered frivolous. There are quaint old monasteries and, at Bethlehem, a tradition of choral singing handed down from father to son by the Moravians. Last but not least there is, if not the costume of the Quaker, the spirit of the Quaker which expresses itself in gentle serenity, moderation and dignity. It is the Quaker spirit that makes Philadelphia a contented community, full of domestic virtue and thrift, brooding benignly over its children despite the impact of increasing industrialization.

Between New York City and Pennsylvania, however, there is still another state. Those travelers who know no more of it than they can observe from a pullman window are inclined to think of New Jersey as a dismal no-man's land, at best a sleeping place for commuters who work in New York and rely on the metropolis for entertainment, stimulation and conviviality. Even one of its native sons, who should know better, the brilliant Edmund Wilson, writes of the "yellow and foundering marshes, the rusty backyards of factories, tangled grooves of railroad tracks, and the greasy black of Newark Bay," ending up by stigmatizing the state as a "dreary dumping-ground of odds and ends not wanted in the cities . . . the doormat of New York." Fortunately there is more to New Jersey than the tarnished disorder of the Hackensack meadows. Even the mildly adventurous, pushing beyond the commuter belt (which is not in itself unprepossessing with its shaded lawns), are rewarded by bits out of American history, quaint old houses, old towns, rolling hills, stretches of beach attractive enough to draw millions of visitors every summer. If they push far enough they will see one of America's little-known areas, the haze-hung pine barrens.

By comparison with the region southwest of New York, the northern hinterland seems more detached, almost remote. It is certain that upstate New Yorkers no more feel that the city

252

of New York belongs to them than does the man from Trenton or even Cleveland. But if New York State is not tied to the metropolis with as close a bond as is Pennsylvania, it is an empire in its own right. And if New York City has something of all the world, New York state has something of all America. From Montauk Point, off the seagoing tip of Long Island, to Lake Erie is four hundred miles, and in between is a wealth of farms, orchards, mountains, forests and lakes.

The heart of this empire is the Hudson River Valley, which played a primordial role in the development of the country. The only inside route from the settlements along the east coast to the St. Lawrence was by way of the Hudson, Lake George and Lake Champlain. The Erie Canal was partly responsible for making New York America's leading city, wresting financial dominance for it from Philadelphia and establishing it as the foremost market place.

Despite its concentrations of industry, much of New York State is rural, and almost at the back door of the world's greatest city one can find farmers plowing with oxen, villages made up of inbred descendants of Hessian soldiers, vineyards where the secrets of wine-making are locked in the expansive bosoms of Italian families. The charm of the state lies in its great rivers and old houses, but he does not truly know it who has not seen the Adirondacks, Lake George, the Finger Lakes region, the Genesee Valley—just as it might have been said in the past that a couple was not truly married if they had not on their honeymoon visited Niagara Falls.

Of the smaller states comprising the second tier, Maryland and Delaware uphold the tradition of dignity and tolerance going back to the days of Lord Calvert and Lord De La Warr. Maryland is a median state in population, value of manufactures, production of natural wealth, in relative importance of its leading city, climate and a host of other factors. H. L. Mencken describes it as "the apex of normalcy," and adds the corollary that it is "dull, depressing, and steadily growing worse." But even the Bad Boy of Baltimore acknowledges the tradition of handsome women, fast horses, and the gracious atmosphere of the old mansions along the Chesapeake, where life had perhaps more charm than even in Virginia.

To the fact that its people were jealous of their prerogatives, what is properly a segment of the eastern half of Maryland owes its existence as a state — Delaware. The Swedish merchant Usselinx reported to King Gustavus Adolphus that it was "a fine land, in which all the necessaries and comforts of life are to be enjoyed in overflowing abundance." The tolerance and cosmopolitanism of the Central Northeast were here founded on the mingling of Swedes, Dutch

253

and English, enhanced by the Quaker spirit of sobriety and decency. Once the fief of a great aristocratic family, Delaware is today just as surely the fief of a great industrial family, the du Ponts, whose giant chemical and explosives industry has given them a strong influence over its economy, education and philanthropy, its organs of opinion, its politics. It may be added that the du Ponts administer their trusteeship in a spirit of *noblesse oblige*.

Quite different from any of the other Central Northeast states is West Virginia, an offspring to which Virginia gave birth during the pangs of the Civil War and, to carry the metaphor further, put out on her back doorstep. It is not surprising that West Virginia should be different, for it is neither truly of the North, South, East or West. Until recently its trackless and beautiful tangle of wilderness was little disturbed by any but the mountaineer, that picturesque and introverted individual who even now may feel impelled to lift up his rifle and send a bullet singing across the valley. But West Virginia today, though still full of scenic charm, may be summed up in one short black word: coal. Its hills are pock-marked with mines, crisscrossed with tracks. Coal lies everywhere like the filling in a giant layer cake. Half the population lives by means of the industry, either directly or indirectly.

It is impossible to discuss the lower tier without including Washington, D. C. And Washington presents an element of interest possessed by no other American city. Cities usually spring up in connection with harbors or waterways, millstreams, crossroads, coaching relays, railroad junctions, mines, foundries, plants. However, the location of the nation's capital was arbitrarily decided on, and the plan of the city itself was conceived in the mind of a French artist of vision, aided by Washington and Jefferson. Long before the swamps were drained and the hills stripped of trees, the location of its avenues, open spaces and important buildings had been fixed.

To see Washington by air on a clear day is to see Major L'Enfant's plan spread out before you. Here is the white dome of the Capitol rising from its surrounding trees, there the gold dome of the Congressional Library; here the Mall, lined with great government buildings, there the shaft in honor of the first President; here the massive porticoes of the memorial to the equally great Lincoln, mirrored in an oblong pool, there the sluggish snake of the Potomac winding out to Alexandria.

Before you lies a city of beauty and exterior calm, reflecting the aspiration of L'Enfant to express the noble and the majestic. Beyond the government buildings are rows of red-brick

254

houses, some typically Georgian, flanking spacious squares and a few stately mansions reminiscent of the true South; for Washington is essentially a Southern city. Unfortunately, even today, there are gaps filled with cheap frame houses, shacks and dilapidated stores, giving the city a slightly dowdy look for all its essential purity. But a greater contrast between its placid charm and the hectic streets of Manhattan would be hard to imagine.

Beyond the production of "issues and slogans," the capital has virtually no industry except the tourist trade, which rivals that of New York. As a result, for all its flurry of activity, it is in a way curiously characterless and lacking in vitality. It is not based on good solid industry, the necessity to yield a profit, to provide a living, to manufacture, produce and exchange. The activity is created, of course, by activities of the government of the United States. Here are the men who are officially running this country, from the President down through the Cabinet members, the Supreme Court judges, the Senators and Representatives, to the gardener on the White House grounds. And around and about them are thousands of representatives of organizations, official and unofficial, who wish to have a part in making the policies according to which the country is governed. Add to this the foreign diplomats who lend a flavor of cosmopolitanism, the wealthy and often astute hostesses who constitute what is left of "society," the generals and admirals, the press, which is present in large numbers to explain or try to explain just what is going on, and one begins to get a picture of turmoil behind the city's facades.

Finally, Washington has another characteristic, stemming from the fact that half of its population is made up of persons who work for the government, or wives, husbands and relatives of persons who work for the government. These are Americans from every section of the country, mainly in the middle or low-to-middle income group, as straightforward as they would be back home. The result is that beneath its veneer of sophistication Washington has the flavor of a big American provincial city like Los Angeles.

All these, from white-haired statesman to bald-headed bureau clerk, from goateed ambassador to beardless Capitol page boy, from beribboned admiral to gray-garbed postman, go to make up Washington. Fortunately the merry-go-round spins in a setting that as cities go is one of the most beautiful, if not the most beautiful, in the Central Northeast and indeed in the United States. L'Enfant's dream at last came true, and the city — on the surface at least — expresses the serenity he would have wished.

255

A monument to America's belief in equal justice under law is the classic Supreme Court Building in Washington. Flanking the Goddess of Liberty in the pediment are Order, Authority, Council and Research. In the building are courtrooms, libraries, offices and press rooms.

Simple classic lines give the White House a charm of design the world has seldom matched. Presidential mansion since 1800, burned in 1814, altered many times, the late eighteenth-century Renaissance building was first officially named "The White House" by Theodore Roosevelt.

Strange and wonderful American ghosts linger in the magnificent East Room of the White House. First Lady Dolly Madison once dried presidential wash here. The Washington portrait she rescued in 1814 hangs on a wall that looked down on great receptions, saw Lincoln lie in state.

George Washington's half brother, Lawrence, built Mount Vernon in 1743, and it remained in the family more than a century. Now one of America's cherished shrines, it contains much of the original furniture as well as many possessions of Washington, whose tomb lies near the house.

The Tomb of the Unknown Soldier in Arlington Cemetery honors First World War dead. Inscribed, "Here rests in honored glory an American Soldier known but to God," it contains the body of a doughboy awarded the Congressional Medal of Honor and high Allied decorations.

The theme of simple grandeur in the capital's shrines continues in the Jefferson Memorial. Jefferson liked spherical architecture, used it both in buildings of the University of Virginia and in Monticello, his home. Classic lines suggest Jefferson's classic love of intellectual freedom.

Generally reminiscent of the Parthenon, the Lincoln Memorial is one of Washington's most imposing monuments. Every year more than a million visitors pass reverently between its Doric columns and stand before the 19-foot-high statue of America's Civil War President.

Bloody Lane at Antietam, in rolling Maryland countryside, saw some of the Civil War's worst fighting. Lee's son was wounded at Antietam. Lincoln visited troops here after the battle.

But old wounds quickly healed, and Maryland hills and meadows soon became the pleasant places they were before the Civil War. The state boasts some of the best steeplechasing country in America and many enthusiastic riders, fox hunters and horse-racing fans.

Colonial Maryland lived graciously and well. Homes like this saw frequent hunt breakfasts, dinners of fried chicken, Chesapeake oysters. Much of Maryland's tradition is Southern.

One of the earliest sparks from the friction that finally flamed into Civil War was struck in Harpers Ferry, West Virginia. On the night of October 16, 1859, John Brown and 22 abolitionist followers seized the federal armory. Two days later, government troops captured Brown

and six others (the remainder were killed or escaped). Brown was tried and hanged for treason in Charles Town. This rugged country, where the Potomac (close foreground) and Shenandoah rivers cut through a narrow gorge, provided an ominously fitting scene for John Brown's raid.

West Virginia's gold-domed state capitol overlooks the Great Kanawha River in Charleston, which began as a frontier fort, is now the industrial center of Kanawha Valley.

Coal gave the Central Northeast its lead in national industry. With the country's greatest coal reserve, West Virginia has produced more bituminous than any other state since the early 1930's. Pennsylvania's output is second. Modern electrical and pneumatic equipment, improved lighting and ventilation have stepped up production and made mining less back-breaking.

Sweeping views over tidy Pennsylvania Dutch farms and little towns, common in east central Pennsylvania, are nowhere better than in the Susquehanna River Valley. From Northumberland, shown here, where the north and west branches of the Susquehanna join, the river flows south through the state capital at Harrisburg and into Chesapeake Bay. William Penn obtained

territory north of here in 1696 from tribes under the Iroquois Confederacy, and English soldiers were given grants of land for fighting in the Pontiac War. Well into the eighteenth century there was commerce by flatboat along the river but, as other transportation developed, shallows and rapids made boats impractical. Main traffic in the valley now goes by highway and railroad.

America's first capitol, Independence Hall, towers above a five-unit statehouse group in Philadelphia. Here Washington received command of the Continental Army, a handful of citizens heard the Declaration of Independence read, and patriots framed the Constitution.

William Penn's house (left), on high ground west of the Schuylkill River in Philadelphia's Fairmount Park, recalls Quaker stock that gave the Quaker City its name and vigor. Iron stove plates in the Bucks County Museum at Doylestown are relics of the equally worthy Dutch.

Benjamin Franklin, printer, scientist, author, statesman, first citizen of Pennsylvania, is commemorated in this marble statue in Philadelphia's Franklin Institute, famous for scientific exhibits. The Liberty Bell stands on a pedestal on the first floor of Independence Hall.

Pittsburgh's smoke means jobs and money for Pennsylvanians, industrial might for the nation. In the Golden Triangle, where the Monongahela and Allegheny rivers join to form the Ohio, are the headquarters of an empire of manufacturing and finance. Pittsburgh makes half the country's steel, coke, plate glass; leads the world in electrical equipment, air brakes . . .

270

. . . cork and other products. The Smoky City ships three times as much by rail as New York or Chicago, has the world's greatest Bessemer steel plant. Heavy industries, like the steel mill shown here, lie along the rivers. The rest of the city spreads over surrounding hills where industrial money has built churches, fine homes, scientific and cultural institutions.

271

At mid-growth America was torn by the Civil War, and the Central Northeast bore its share of suffering. Marking the battlefield where 50,000 fell as casualties and Lincoln made his deathless speech of tribute and dedication is the Gettysburg National Military Park.

In this trim little Pennsylvania farm house, America weathered an earlier crisis. During the winter of 1777-78, while the British lived royally in Philadelphia, Washington and his lean Continental Army shivered in the hills of Valley Forge, only 20 miles away.

At Lititz in Pennsylvania's Lancaster County, a Mennonite farmer and his wife watch progress at a country sale. Calling themselves "Plain People," sometimes called Pennsylvania German but most often (and more properly) Pennsylvania Dutch, these shy but shrewd and self-respecting folk make smooth cheeses, spiced scrapple and sausage, run farms with great skill.

274

Tidiness bespeaks the diligence of Pennsylvania Dutch. Barns often carry paintings. Many are larger than the one shown, are painted red, marked with "hex signs" to ward off witchcraft.

Spice grinders like the one held by the traditionally garbed Amish boy are still common. Old ways persist among the Amish, who send their children to one-room schools, have even moved to avoid using consolidated schools. But America has no more industrious farmers.

Rare colonial charm balances Delaware's industrial strength. Here, in New Castle, Immanuel Church and churchyard have mellowed since the early eighteenth century. Before being deeded to William Penn in 1682, the region had changed sovereignty five times . . .

... and changing sovereigns left varied marks. Among New Castle's finest examples of Georgian Colonial architecture are the George Read house (left) and the old courthouse.

Anglican church plan dictated the tower and spire on Immanuel Church, whereas the Dutch colonists, who took New Castle from the Swedes in 1655, built snug, wide-eaved houses.

New Jersey has a spectacular variety of its own. Besides the Palisades, shown here, are salt marshes, pine barrens, fishing villages, truck farms, cranberry bogs, shaded colonial homes, great universities, factories and famous vacation resorts. Table flat in the south, its northern

counties cover wooded hills and reach east to a dramatic stop at the Palisades. At this point, near Alpine, the cliff rises sheer about 500 feet above the Hudson River. Farther south, the Palisades face the heaped-up, glinting miracle of Manhattan.

As part of its claim to importance in the industrial Central Northeast, New Jersey offers large oil refineries. This fractionating tower at Elizabeth separates petroleum components.

But New Jersey's best-known business is recreation. Hunters who set decoys in Barnegat Bay near Forked River also find these waters ideal for swimming, fishing and small-boat sailing. An inland waterway runs nearly the entire length of the Jersey coast, from Cape May to Sandy Hook, is beaded with summer resorts that make the state one of the nation's favorite playgrounds.

281

Known around the world, Atlantic City's boardwalk is the Broadway of American vacation resorts. Its 60-foot-wide plank surface runs four miles along the beach, past linen shops and shooting galleries, swank haberdasheries, penny arcades, drugstores and salt-water taffy shops.

In boardwalk stores and in plants, offices and hotels behind them, Atlantic City's 100,000 do business with more than 16 million visitors a year. Summer is the busy season, but a mild climate and vast accommodations make it a year-round resort and convention city.

New York State reaches north and west of its greatest city to include an empire of farms, lakes, mountains, cities and the scenes of some of America's finest legends. Shown here is Sleepy Hollow Cemetery, near Tarrytown, where Washington Irving lived and wrote his mellow tales of Dutch settlers, Rip Van Winkle, the Headless Horseman and bony Ichabod Crane.

The Hudson Valley is full of Dutch names: Poughkeepsie, Staatsburg, Claverack. In this Dutch colonial house at Rensselaer, Dutchman Richard Schuckburg wrote *Yankee Doodle*.

285

Under summer sun or winter ice, Niagara Falls is among scenic New York's grandest sights. Taken from the excursion steamer *Maid of the Mist,* this picture shows the 167-foot American falls. Luna Island (right) is a favorite lookout point for honeymooners and visitors.

New York state out-farms most of the other 47, growing potatoes as valuable as Idaho's, more hay than all New England. It has led the nation in beets and cabbages, follows only Wisconsin and Minnesota in dairying. This farm is in Rensselaer County, near the Vermont line.

Washington recommended founding West Point in 1776, but it did not open until 1802. Since then it has trained cadets in a course of rigid military discipline, balanced with athletics and academic studies. Graduating second lieutenants hold bachelor of science degrees.

The seagoing tip of New York state is Montauk Point on the outer end of Long Island. Near Montauk Light, built in 1796, are wind-blown Montauk State Park and the little fishing village of Montauk. From the flounder run in March until winter storms add fury to bleakness, the waters hereabouts are a rendezvous for anglers after tuna and swordfish.

Long Island Sound, sheltered between the island and the mainland, offers some of the nation's best boating water for racing sloops, power cruisers, even outboard-driven skiffs.

New York's fabulous Manhattan Island lies between the Hudson (left) and East rivers, with the Harlem River completing its water boundary. Mid-town skyscrapers lie just south of Central Park; clustered towers of the financial district cover the island's tip.

Behind the ferry slips and Battery Park on lower Manhattan rise the staffed spires of two of the world's four tallest buildings: the Manhattan Company Building and 60 Wall Tower (right). In the distance are the other two, the Empire State and the needle-sharp Chrysler buildings.

In the statue of Minerva and the Bell Ringers, City Hall's graceful flying staircase . . .

. . . the entrance to Riverside Church and the tower of the Chrysler Building, New York has . . .

. . . a finely drawn beauty. Other sights are the harbor's Statue of Liberty, and Grant's Tomb . . .

. . . the Stock Exchange and the 1,250-foot Empire State Building, tallest in the world.

293

New York has variety in the Bohemian crowding of Greenwich Village, Third Avenue shops . . .

. . . the Cloisters (restoration of a twelfth-century monastery) and humming Times Square.

On Park Avenue and Central Park Lake, the city vibrates to an ever-changing theme. From

Bowery barber shops to wharves on the East River, its face is always different, often new.

Among New York's wonders is the RCA Building in Rockefeller Center. Called Radio City by most New Yorkers, the center includes 14 buildings between Fifth and the Avenue of the Americas, Forty-eight and Fifty-first streets. Besides an outdoor skating rink, there are restaurants, broadcasting studios, publishing offices and a tremendous theater where . . .

. . . the Radio City Music Hall Rockettes brighten each week's stage show with precision dancing that sets chorus standards for the world. Sharing the giant stage are the Hall's *corps de ballet* and a glee club, assisted by a 65-piece orchestra. With a total staff of 600, the Music Hall produces elaborate shows in the theatrical and musical capital of America.

Exchange Place runs east from Broadway, a block south of Wall Street, in lower Manhattan's financial district. Narrow streets between canyon-walled buildings at the heart of this financial empire accentuate the vertical construction New York had to adopt to provide living, working and playing space for nearly two million people on an island only 12½ miles long.

The Third Avenue El (only elevated remaining) meshes with a vast surface, water and underground transit system to provide transportation in the business capital of the world.

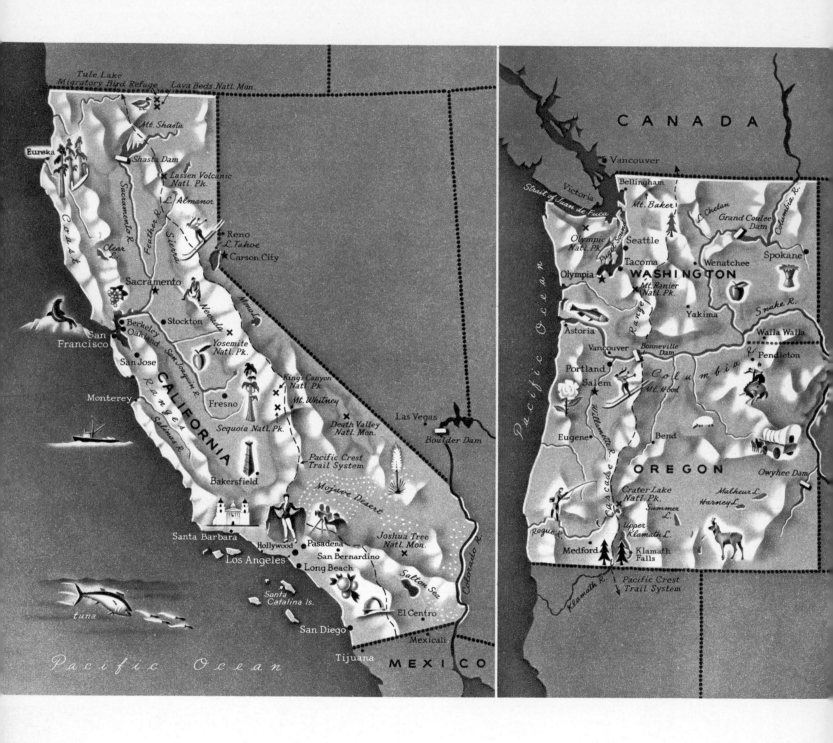

Coastal Contrasts

THE NORTHERN HALF of the Pacific Coast is a land of water. The great Cascade range sheers up to catch the rain clouds from the Pacific and spills them on its spruce-clad escarpments. For days on end, the Washington, Oregon, and northern California seaboard is mantled in drizzling rain.

The southern half of the Pacific Coast is a land of sun. The tawny hills and the beaches of Southern California are, for days on end, floodlighted with brilliant sunshine.

The contrast does not end there. Despite its rich potentialities, the Northwest is still sparsely settled and mainly rural. But the dazzling reputation of Southern California has already attracted so many admirers that it is relatively crowded, and there are indications that the Los Angeles region may grow into one of the greatest metropolitan centers of all time.

Again, the Northwest is more conscious of its past, distinctively American, representatively pioneer, bound up with what is perhaps the most romantic of the covered-wagon traditions — the Oregon Trail. San Francisco, which for most purposes can be considered a northern city, is proud of its gold rush. To be the descendant of a forty-niner is the equivalent in San Francisco of claiming, in Boston, ancestors who came over on the *Mayflower.* But Southern California, despite a heritage of architecture, color, music and gaiety from the days of the Spanish explorers, is too new to be so conscious of historical perspective. In the horde of sun-worshippers there are few who were actually born in the state, and ten years' residence suffices to make one an old-timer.

The pattern of contrast between coastal regions is repeated on a lesser scale in the state of California itself. Within a hundred miles of each other are to be found the highest point in the United States, Mt. Whitney which towers 14,495 feet above sea level, and Bad Water,

301

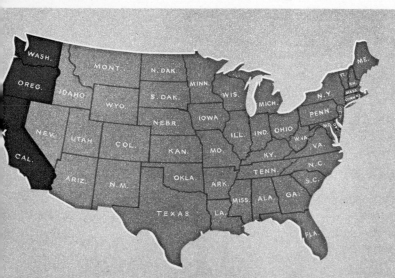

in Death Valley, which slinks down like some prehistoric reptile, 279.8 feet below sea level. The searing, blighting heat of Death Valley gives it the highest temperature in the country, whereas Californians claim that parts of the High Sierras have the greatest fall of snow.

This huge state, second largest in the Union, with her two great cities more widely separated than are New York and Montreal, offers a host of paradoxes.

The southern part has valleys that are fertile without rivers, rivers without water, deserts that bloom with flowers, wet seasons without rain, dry seasons with showers, rats that climb trees and squirrels that nest in the ground. It was of Southern California that Mark Twain was thinking when he wrote that he "fell into a river and came out all dusty." Although California is the westernmost state, the Pacific port of Los Angeles is east of Reno, Nevada, and Agua Caliente, a few score miles inland, is east of Coeur d'Alene in Idaho. California has orchards growing south of orange groves and the flora of two zones on opposite sides of a mountain pass. Motion-picture directors boast they can duplicate the Sahara, the African veldt, the Alps and the Riviera virtually at their doorstep. The state has the vines of France, the oil fields of the Persian Gulf. It has the oldest and largest living tree in the world, the largest young metropolis. Almost within a day's drive in a movie star's sport model, the region can provide anything from a glacier to an active volcano.

In addition to some of the most beautiful national parks in the country, with facilities for camping and fishing, the snowy Sierras have an exceptionally long skiing season which every year attracts thousands of winter-sports enthusiasts. Although this galaxy of scenic effects — plus such attractions as the race tracks at Santa Anita and Tanforan, golf courses of the caliber of Pebble Beach — has proved irresistible to visitors from other regions, there are other anomalies less to the taste of a chamber of commerce propagandist. Along with the largest per capita income and the highest standard of living in the country, California has the running sore of its migrant labor problem. Its showy mansions are balanced by decrepit shacks. And the very persons who stage elaborate fiestas are careful to keep the Mexicans on the other side of the railroad tracks. High standards in scholarship and research are balanced by a susceptibility to strange cults and freakish revivals. Like its scentless flowers, many of the region's creeds do not have the odor of sanctity. The Garden of Eden is full of hot-dog stands purveying the most authentic varieties of baloney.

Still the list of contradictions is not closed. Urbanites live in the country; rural hicks live

302

within sound of the screech of trolley cars. Farms are run like factories. Los Angeles, optimistic over continuing growth, wrinkles its nose at solid, progressive San Francisco.

Vociferous feuds, nevertheless, supply an outlet for the heat generated by some of these divergencies—feuds between northern half and southern half, between farmers and city-dwellers, between prospectors and desert rats.

It is not surprising that a region of violent extremes should breed a spirit of exuberance in its inhabitants, since if by any chance the course of events tends to degenerate into the hum-drum, nature herself lends a hand in the form of a forest fire, a flood, a landslide, or a baby earthquake (the last euphemistically baptized a temblor). Californians, someone has said, "irri-gate, cultivate, and exaggerate."

One element only, in the kaleidoscope, shows no tendency to extremes, and its very uniformity has spelled the success of Southern California. Warmed by the Pacific, shut off from the cold by the Sierras, the region is climatically an island, with enough water to keep the atmosphere temperate and not too much to prevent its being dry. There results an equable, benign climate enough like that of Tahiti or the Marquesas to satisfy the displaced sons of Kansas. One way and another it has brought more wealth to California than ever she dug out of the ground in the days of the gold rush. It annually attracts two million visitors who spend three hundred million dollars. (A like amount is spent by Californians themselves who also relish the state's scenic variety.) Since many of the visitors could not long resist its Circe-like spell, the climate was also responsible for the area's real-estate boom. With Florida, California is the fastest growing state. The sun brought the lavish, opulent and fantastic movie industry. It ripened the fruit in the citrus groves, so that despite California's pre-eminence in other fields, agriculture remains one of her leading income producers.

The sun ripened the crops, but the crops would not have been there without water, and the water would not have been there without elaborately conceived and executed public works. California leads all states in irrigation. Over five million acres of primary land have been irri-gated at a capital investment of over three hundred million dollars. Developed water power totals two and a half million horsepower. A man-made water supply brought to life the great truck-garden valleys—the Salinas, San Joaquin, Santa Clara and Sacramento, and the Imperial Valley to the south. In addition to citrus fruits, these produce apples, pears, lettuce, plums, prunes, peaches, cantaloupes, apricots, olives and walnuts. The sun, however, can be given

303

credit for the wines of the Napa, Livermore and other hillsides which in soil and climatic requirements approximate the vineyards of Bordeaux and Burgundy.

To complete the score of the sun's benefactions, one should not overlook the psychological effect of the climate which prompts the visitor to begin by shedding most of his clothes and end by shedding most of his inhibitions. "The lands of the sun," reads a Spanish proverb, "expand the soul."

And, in interpreting California, Spanish proverbs come not inappropriately to mind. The picturesqueness of the setting is not solely attributable to purple mountains, gray-green olive groves, and iridescent ocean. The Spaniards and early Mexicans, with their graceful religious and secular architecture, their almost childish delight in dancing and singing and gay costumes, their fiestas and barbecues and rodeos, have bequeathed a colorful heritage.

For California does in a very real sense have a past, even if the modern scene bears little relation to it. The story of its beginnings is romantic. Passing over the Indians who, though they were more numerous in California than anywhere else on the continent, vanished almost without leaving a trace, it begins with Juan Cabrillo, a Portuguese navigator who explored the coast in the sixteenth century, only to be followed a few years later by the dashing Sir Francis Drake. Afterward, coastal valleys remained undisturbed until a frail but indomitable Franciscan missionary, Father Junipero Serra, at about the time America was severing ties with Britain, flung a chain of missions all up and down the coast. The missions are still there, and against a background of mountain, coast and sea, palm, vine and garden, glow with a gem-like beauty. After the era of the missions came the day of the great ranch owners, when land was dispensed with such prodigality by the Spanish and Mexican governors that by the eighteen thirties a few families owned most of the territory.

The story of the conquest of California by the Americans and the subsequent discovery of gold at Sutter's Mill, luring thousands of eager treasure-seekers from all over the country and even from the far corners of the world in one of the greatest stampedes of history, is too well known to retell here. However, attention should be called to the fact that partly due to the gold rush the West Coast was one of our early frontiers. As they made their way west, the pioneers dropped off and settled wherever the land was fertile. But when they reached the great plains and desert wastes, they simply kept going until their persistence finally brought them once more to a propitious soil. The frontier, which was Ohio and Kentucky in 1820, was

304

California and Oregon in 1850. The intervening regions were not settled until much later.

The same desert barrier had its effect on the psychology of the Westerners because it isolated them from the rest of the country much as the Atlantic had cut the colonists off from England. It is not hard to find Californians who can remember when the first transcontinental trains reached Sacramento and, of course, when the first automobiles laboriously ploughed their way from New York. With this geographical separateness, the Coast has been less under the influence of national opinion than any other region.

In fact, despite obvious and violent growing pains, one can sense the possibility of some kind of spontaneous and indigenous cultural development taking place there. Already the West Coast has attracted Thomas Mann, who does not write for the movies; Aldous Huxley, weaned from polite decadence to mysticism; Gerald Heard, Stravinsky, and other front rank creative minds.

Los Angeles, with 451 square miles of far-flung residential, business and entertainment areas intended for people with cars — and only for people with cars — is already the largest single municipality in the world in area. A third of the state's entire population lives there. And this, the mushroom growth of no more than a few decades, is only a beginning.

As is well known, industrialists of the Far West are engaged in a battle to wrest independence from industrialists of the East. They have an airplane industry. They have war-developed steel plants rivaling in importance those of the East and South. It would not be rash to prophesy that they will win their battle. For this reason and because of the lure of the climate, Southern California expects to continue to grow as other regions slip into senescence. With its habitual optimism, it expects some day to have a population of thirty millions — a challenging conception. In time the entire region from the mountains to the sea may be one great city.

As you push farther up the coast, you leave behind the exotic, the bizarre, and the flamboyant. Hill-girt San Francisco relishes her rowdy past with considerable gusto, but is old enough and settled enough to be dignified about it. San Franciscans are secure in their conviction that their city is one of the most stimulating and cosmopolitan in the world. And by the time you get to Washington and Oregon, the vagaries of a land that is little more than one huge movie set have faded. Conflicting influences are shed in the sanity of the great woods, before the majesty of snow-tipped peaks, the glitter of inland waterways and rushing rivers, the repose of fertile valleys and the restraining cloak of the creeping fog and the soft drizzle of rain.

305

The Pacific Northwest comprises a hundred and fifty thousand square miles of dank evergreens, swamps, pasture land, mountainous crags, wind-swept plains and wheat fields. It is not a difficult region to understand. It has a great mountain chain: the Cascades. It has a great river: the Columbia. It has a great waterway: Puget Sound. The towering barrier of the Cascades splits both Washington and Oregon into the northwest of high arid ranges and wheat fields on the east, and the humid slopes that descend to the Pacific on the west. On the eastern side of the division the hardworking Northwesterners go in for cattle and sheep raising, and for prospecting and mining. Much of the farm land here is irrigated. On the west they are loggers, captains of seagoing ships and river craft, prospectors and, again, miners. Farming here is carried on in well-watered pastures where placid milch cows can find plenty of succulent fodder.

Next consider the Columbia which, with its countless tributaries, has as its basin the entire Northwest and more; for, in addition to all of Washington, it serves most of Oregon and Idaho, northwestern Montana and parts of Nevada, Utah and Wyoming. This area produces a third of the nation's lumber and a third of its apples. The Northwest, according to one authority, also produces a quarter of the country's wool, a quarter of its silver, a fifth of its wheat, a sixth of its lead, an eighth of its salmon. In the Grand Coulee Dam it has what has been called the greatest engineering project ever undertaken by man, which is expected to reclaim enough land to provide at least 25,000 farms.

Finally, there is Puget Sound, the greatest inland sea on the North American continent, with long fingers clutching at the great forests between the Cascades and the mountains of the coast. Only sixty-five miles in length, its minutely subdivided and indented shore-line is said to measure 1,800 miles. All the fleets in the world could shelter here. No matter how much the Northwest grows, it will never lack adequate harbor facilities.

The story of the Northwest is as American in flavor as the smell of the sawdust in its logging camps. It was "born at the hands of the pioneers and weaned with the gold of California." The United States and Britain nearly went to war for possession of it but wisely thought better, and it is actually the only part of what is now the United States that we didn't have to fight for or purchase.

Names such as Juan de Fuca Straits, Cape Ferrelo, Cape Blanco and Cape Perpetua, San Juan and Lopez islands testify that the Spaniards visited this coast in far-off days. So did Drake. Shortly before 1800 the region was explored from the sea by Captain Robert Grey. A few years

later Lewis and Clark crossed the wilderness from the Missouri and by following the Columbia from the mountain barrier to the river's mouth charted a gateway to the new West. They were followed after a brief interval by John Jacob Astor's fur-scouting expedition which, after many difficulties, also reached the mouth of the Columbia and founded Astoria. For the next half century, on the heels of hunters and trappers, came a tide of immigrants, their prairie schooners raising pillars of dust, their cattle stumbling through lava plains; immigrants who braved Indians, exhaustion, famine, and who, to get their women and children across rivers, took the wheels off their prairie schooners and made them into something more closely resembling their seagoing prototype. There followed a pageant of hunters, trappers, prospectors, lumberjacks, fishermen, sailors, cowboys, outlaws, sheriffs, hermits, desperadoes. Later settlers, steadier and perhaps more industrious if not so colorful, were drawn by free land, mineral resources, farming and stock raising. Although the Union Pacific spanned the continent in 1869, the Northwest had to do without an iron substitute for the Oregon Trail until 1883, when Henry Villard completed the Northern Pacific. Railroad construction brought settlers in increasing numbers. The latest development by which the Northwest continues to exert a pull on inhabitants of other regions is the reclamation of vast areas and the furnishing of plentiful hydroelectric power by means of the greatest dams in the world. The Northwest, abounding in natural wealth, remains a land of tremendous potentialities.

It is also a land of tall timber, tall men—and tall tales. Not for nothing was it the scene of one of the best-known legends of Paul Bunyan, whose Blue Ox, Babe, you remember, dug most of Puget Sound by dragging an Alaskan glacier across the northwest corner of the United States. In 1883 *Harper's Magazine* reported: "They have discovered footprints three feet long in the sands of Oregon, supposed to belong to a lost race." And it has been stated on good authority that the land of Brobdingnag in *Gulliver's Travels,* which was the land of giants, was patterned by Swift on an explorer's description of the Olympic Peninsula.

The resident of the Northwest is never far from great mountains. There is a resultant effect on his character. Men of this region have stability, yet are refreshingly free from stereotypes. The majestic natural setting contributes repose and dignity to human existence. For it is not hope of gain alone that attracts people to the Northwest. There is a pull in the scenery. Mountain crests and the tops of giant trees draw the gaze upward; surf-lashed rocks carry it out to sea; there is the hint of further enchantment around a bend in a climbing highway or a great rolling river.

The lofty, snow-capped Cascade range runs south from Canada across Washington and Oregon, dividing each state into two characteristic areas: the rain-drenched, heavily wooded coastal slopes and the dry but fertile plateau east of the mountains. Mount Shuksan (above) in Washington, rising to an elevation of 9,038 feet, defied the efforts of all climbers until 1906.

308

Approximately 75 miles southwest of Spokane, industrial metropolis of Washington's plateau country, the 198-foot Palouse Falls are on the site of a proposed state park.

In 1945, nearly half the United States apple crop was grown in Washington — 25,840,000 bushels, valued at over $75,000,000. Found mainly in the Wenatchee and Yakima river valleys, the orchards yield the state's biggest crop, leading such other agricultural produce as wheat, barley, oats, corn, potatoes, pears, peaches, peas and hops, as well as sheep and cattle.

Ice-tipped Mount Rainier, with an altitude of 14,408 feet, dominates Mount Rainier National Park, is the third highest peak in the country. It is a favorite among mountain climbers.

Summer recreation in Washington centers around Puget Sound—her great "inland sea"—where regattas range from dinghy competitions to the annual Seattle-British Columbia races.

A gigantic cataract, many times the size of Niagara, was stilled during the Ice Age when the Columbia River shifted its course. All that remains of this ancient falls, which dropped 417 feet along a three-mile rim, are the pocked walls in Washington's Dry Falls State Park.

Coastline or forest, plateau or river bed — all of Washington is dominated by her massive, snow-whitened peaks. Mount Baker, with its 12 glaciers and more than 44 square miles of ice fields, presents but one example of the state's scenic wonders.

313

Washington ranks second in lumber output. In 1943, the state's camps like this in Olympic National Forest produced 13 per cent of the U. S. total of thirty-four billion board feet.

Felling trees, stripping and sawing them for shipment all over the world demands a special skill and daring. Logrolling contests, like the one pictured above, long ago developed as a natural outlet for the hardy spirit of lumberjacks isolated for months in Washington's vast forests of Douglas fir, yellow pine, white pine, spruce, larch and cedar.

Forming most of the boundary between Washington and Oregon, the Columbia River winds across the former's eastern plateau, through the Cascade Mountains and the rolling Coast Range to the Pacific Ocean. Upstream from Portland, Oregon, the Columbia River Highway

passes the modified English Tudor Crown Point Vista House (on bluff at right) 725 feet above the water. Seventeen miles east of Crown Point, Bonneville Dam spans the Columbia, forming a huge reservoir which has submerged many historic and scenic spots.

Oregon possesses varied and picturesque landscapes. Along the coast, with its rolling fog banks and moderate climate, beaches stretch between precipitous boulders jutting out from the sea. Sir Francis Drake explored this region in the latter half of the sixteenth century.

Farther inland the terrain rises through rolling hills to the Cascade Mountains. Heavy rainfall has made dairying prosperous in the valleys. Along navigable rivers like the Rogue, pictured above, stern-wheelers once carried a busy passenger and freight traffic.

318

A vast interior plateau stretches eastward in Oregon from the Cascades to the Blue Mountains. Here moderate rainfall and broad areas of flat land made wheat the first crop of westward-moving pioneers. Modern farming methods have kept it the state's principal crop.

Oregon's most spectacular scenic feature is perpetually snow-capped Mount Hood. Rising 11,245 feet amid the Cascades east of Portland, it overlooks one of the state's chief recreational areas — with resorts, ski runs, hiking trails and saddle routes.

The state capitol at Salem, Oregon, is surrounded by two parks containing more than 400 varieties of trees. Replacement for a building destroyed by fire in 1935, it is modern inside and out. Atop its fluted, cylindrical dome stands the heroic figure of "The Pioneer," a reminder of the vision and courage of men and women who settled the state.

Long before the first white men reached Oregon, Indians scooped salmon from the John Day River at Celilo Falls, as they do today under exclusive, perpetual treaty rights.

Crater Lake, high in the Cascade Mountains, has been called one of the three great scenic wonders of the world. A crater within a crater, it rests atop prehistoric Mount Mazama, but its manner of origin is unknown. Under a clear sky its surface is a brilliant aquamarine.

Indian legends refer to Crater Lake as a site where angry gods staged terrifying battles among themselves. Six miles in diameter, 2,000 feet deep, without visible inlet or outlet, the lake is surrounded by towering masses of volcanic ash and broken by tree-strewn Wizard Island.

Here shown where it cuts across Neahkahnie Mountain at a point 500 feet above the water's edge, the Oregon Coast Highway keeps the Pacific in view for almost its entire length.

The 125-foot Astor Column at Astoria depicts the exploration of the Columbia River and the founding of the town. A spiral staircase leads to the observation platform at the top.

California — the promised land to the pioneers — has a jagged coast line broken by three great natural ports at San Francisco, San Diego and Monterey and the man-made port of Los Angeles. Here at Midway Point on Monterey Bay stands the much-photographed Lone Cypress.

Near California's eastern border stretch the towering Sierra Nevadas on whose western slope lies Yosemite National Park. Upper Yosemite Falls, nine times as tall as Niagara, is the highest free-falling cascade in the world, 1,430 feet. The lower fall is 320 feet.

The San Fernando Valley houses four movie studios, three major airports, an automobile assembly plant and miles of citrus groves. Actually a part of Los Angeles, the valley provides, in its 212 square miles, sites for the homes and farms of 165,000 people.

Southeast of Los Angeles, in the Coachella Valley, grow California's dates. Protected by burlap or paper bags, requiring heavy irrigation, they ripen amid such exotic settings as the one above. Approximately 5,000 short tons of dates are grown in California yearly.

For more than four centuries California has felt the influence of far places. The Japanese settled in Los Angeles' "Little Tokyo." To San Francisco the Chinese brought their own customs and methods of worship. The Kong Chow Temple, whose altar is shown above, is the largest Chinese joss house in America and one of two open to the public in San Francisco's Chinatown.

California's first settlers were the Spanish, whose descendants built such missions as San Juan Batista (left) near Monterey, the largest in the state, and San Carlos Barromeo del Rio Carmelo (right) at Carmel, whose wooden cross marks the grave of its founder.

Santa Barbara Mission, at Santa Barbara, is the best preserved of all California missions. A rich combination of Spanish and Moorish design, it is architecturally one of the finest in the state, and the only one whose altar light has shone continuously since its founding, in 1815. A previous building, built in 1786, was destroyed by an earthquake in 1812.

Just north of the Mexican border, the Imperial Dam diverts water into the All-American Canal on the California side of the Colorado River, and into the Gravity Main Canal in Arizona. Part of the Boulder Dam system, the Imperial is 3,430 feet long and 45 feet high.

The Golden Gate Bridge, crossing San Francisco Bay, has the longest single span in the world. It is to the West Coast what the Statue of Liberty is to the East — a welcome to America.

Cahuenga Pass leads a ten-lane highway and the Southern Pacific railway tracks from the flat, fertile San Fernando Valley through the Santa Monica Mountains into bustling Hollywood.

Hollywood is best known for its movie industry. As part of the business of film-making, everything from suburban homes to crashing airplanes is reproduced in miniature and photographed on such indoor stages as the one shown above. Hollywood and nearby Culver City, Beverly Hills, Burbank and North Hollywood produce nearly all of the nation's films.

Californians claim that nowhere else on the globe is outdoor living and playing more fun than in the Golden State. They base this claim on the fact that no spot in California is more than 225 airline miles from the ocean, that the sun *does* shine 355 days of the year and that temperatures — even during the winter — seldom fall below 46 degrees.

336

Californians also boast that, in their land of sunshine, winter sports are as close as the nearest mountain. Above, skiers gather on a slope of Snow Valley, near Big Bear City.

337

More than 20,000 years ago, grinding glacial masses of the Ice Age left in their wake a seven-mile-long, mile-wide trough known today as Yosemite Valley. To many it is the most familiar view in California's Yosemite National Park, so often has it been photographed. Yet it comprises

less than one hundredth of the park's total area stretching down the western side of the Sierra Nevadas. Clouds sweep the rim 3,000 feet above the valley's floor. Its walls rise sharply to such towering peaks as El Capitan, Half Dome and Glacier Point.

Untitled Pictures

Picture Credits

Lines from Cornhuskers, *by Carl Sandburg, are quoted on page 110 by permission of Henry Holt and Company, publishers.*

Look At America

BY THE EDITORS OF LOOK

Maps drawn by R. M. Chapin.
Set in Garamond No. 3 by Riegert & Kennedy, Inc.
Offset plates by Graphic Arts Corporation of Ohio
Color printed in offset by The Kellogg & Bulkeley Co.
Monotone printed in gravure by R. R. Donnelley & Sons Co.

PUBLISHED BY

HOUGHTON MIFFLIN COMPANY

This book was produced by the LOOK Picture Book Division, Cowles Magazines, Inc.: Mildred Barish, Dorothy Castro, Lynn Chase, Jeanette Collins, Ruth Davis, Anne Ehrenberger, Jane Fishlock, Muriel Franceschina, James Fyfe, Ruth Groves, Mary Anne Guitar, Anthony Guyther, Phyllis Hebberd, Amy Hodel, Ruth Imler, Sarah Jordan, Margaret Kander, Patricia Lauber, David Landman, Louis Mercier, Stanley Nevola, Charles Parker, Dale Rooks, Marjorie Rosmarin, Noah Sarlat, Thomas Stanton, Mabel Sweat, Arthur Train, Nancy Ward, Ellen Wivegg.

Under the supervision of: Harry Shaw, Director; James Hosking, Executive Editor; Howard Jensen, Art Editor; Charles C. Moffat, Production Manager; Edmund Motyka and John K. Murphy, Managing Editors.

FOR COWLES MAGAZINES, INC.

Gardner Cowles, President

John Cowles, Chairman of the Board
James S. Milloy, Vice-President
John F. Harding, General Counsel

Harlan Logan, Editor & General Manager
Marvin C. Whatmore, Business Manager
Andrew Hepburn, Travel Editor